SHIMBA
BIBLE STUDY SERIES

THE DIVINITY OF JESUS

GENESIS

Dr. Maxwell Shimba

Printed in the United States of America

TABLE OF CONTENTS

Introduction vi

Chapter 01 1

The Divine Nature of Jesus 1

Chapter 02 15

The Pre-Existence of Jesus................................15

Chapter 03 33

Jesus in Creation..33

Chapter 04 52

Jesus as the Promised Savior 52

Chapter 05 76

The "I Am" Statements of Jesus........................76

Chapter 06 94

Jesus as the Seed of Abraham 94

Chapter 07 114

The Sacfrifice of Isaac and Jesus 114

Chapter 08 130

The Concept of Substitutionary Atonement 130

Chapter 09 159

Joseph as a Type of Christ 159

Chapter 10 186

Jesus as the Fulfillment of the Law..................186

Chapter 11 213

Jesus' Role in Bringing About the New Creation 213

Chapter 12 235

Conclusion..235

Appendices 257

Appendix A.. 257

Appendix B.. 271

Glossary of Theological Terms 271

Appendix C.. 276

Further Reading and Study Questions........................ 276

Bibliography.. 281

Books on the Divinity of Jesus 281

INTRODUCTION

Introduction

The Divinity of Jesus in Genesis

By Dr. Maxwell Shimba

From the opening words of Genesis to the final revelations in the New Testament, the Bible presents a cohesive and intricate tapestry of God's redemptive plan, woven together through the person of Jesus Christ. This book, "The Divinity of Jesus in Genesis," embarks on a profound exploration of how the divine nature and mission of Jesus are embedded within the very foundation of the biblical narrative, beginning with the first book of the Bible.

Purpose of the Book

The primary purpose of this book is to illuminate the divine identity of Jesus Christ as revealed in the book of Genesis. By examining key passages and their theological implications, we seek to uncover the depth and richness of God's revelation of His Son from the very beginning of creation. This exploration not only affirms the continuity of the biblical narrative but also enhances our understanding of Jesus' role in God's redemptive plan.

Structure of the Book

This book is organized into twelve chapters, each delving into specific aspects of Jesus' divinity and His connection to Genesis. The chapters are as follows:

1. Jesus' Divine Nature and Mission - An introduction to the theological framework for understanding Jesus' divinity and mission as outlined in the Scriptures.

2. Jesus in Creation - An exploration of Jesus' role as the divine Word through whom all things were made, linking Genesis 1 with John 1.

3. Jesus as the Promised Seed - A detailed examination of Genesis 3:15, the protoevangelium, and its fulfillment in Jesus.

4. Jesus and the Covenants - How the covenants with Abraham, Isaac, and Jacob foreshadow the coming of Christ and the establishment of the New Covenant.

5. The Prefiguration of Jesus in the Life of Joseph - Parallels between Joseph's life and Jesus' life, suffering, and exaltation.

6. Jesus as the Fulfillment of the Law - Understanding how Jesus fulfills the Mosaic Law and the

prophets, bringing completeness to the Old Testament Scriptures.

7. Jesus and the New Creation - Insights into how Jesus initiates the new creation, transforming individuals and ultimately renewing all of creation.

8. Jesus' Sacrificial Role - Analyzing the sacrificial system in Genesis and its ultimate fulfillment in the sacrificial death of Jesus.

9. The Hope of Redemption - Exploring the themes of hope and restoration found in Genesis and how they point to the ultimate redemption in Christ.

10. Jesus as the Only Savior - Affirming the exclusivity of Jesus as the mediator and redeemer, fulfilling God's promise of salvation.

11. Encouragement to Seek a Deeper Relationship with Jesus - Encouraging believers to deepen their relationship with Christ, recognizing Him as the fulfillment of God's promises.

12. Conclusion - Summarizing the key points and reinforcing the significance of understanding Jesus' divinity and His connection to Genesis.

Theological Foundations

This study is grounded in a Christocentric reading of the Scriptures, recognizing Jesus as the fulfillment of the Law and the Prophets. It employs a typological approach, identifying how various figures and events in Genesis prefigure Christ. Additionally, this book draws on the rich tradition of biblical exegesis and theological reflection, offering insights from church fathers, contemporary theologians, and biblical scholars.

Invitation to the Reader

As you embark on this journey through the pages of Genesis, I invite you to open your heart and mind to the profound truths about Jesus Christ that have been woven into the fabric of Scripture from the very beginning. My hope is that this exploration will not only deepen your understanding of the Bible but also enrich your relationship with Jesus, the eternal Word made flesh.

In the words of the Apostle Paul, "I keep asking that the God of our Lord Jesus Christ, the glorious Father, may give you the Spirit of wisdom and revelation, so that you may know him better" (Ephesians 1:17, NIV). May this study guide you into a deeper knowledge of Christ and His divine role in God's eternal plan.

Dr. Maxwell Shimba
Shimba Theological Institute

DR. MAXWELL SHIMBA

CHAPTER 01

THE DIVINE NATURE OF JESUS

Purpose and Structure of the Book

The purpose of this book is to explore and illuminate the profound connection between Jesus Christ and the foundational truths found in the book of Genesis. By examining the teachings, divinity, and identity of Jesus as the Savior and the "I Am," we aim to uncover the divine threads woven throughout the Scriptures that reveal the consistent and unchanging nature of God's plan for humanity. This book seeks to deepen the reader's understanding of Jesus' divine nature and His pivotal role in both the Old and New Testaments, demonstrating that He is the fulfillment of God's promises from the very beginning.

Purpose

1. Revealing Jesus' Divinity: One of the central aims of this book is to demonstrate that Jesus is not merely a historical figure or a great teacher but the eternal Son of God. His divine nature is evident throughout the Scriptures, and this book will highlight key passages that affirm His deity.

2. Connecting Old and New Testaments: Many believers view the Old and New Testaments as distinct and separate narratives. This book seeks to bridge that gap by showing how Jesus is intricately linked to the Old Testament, particularly Genesis, which lays the foundation for understanding His mission and identity.

3. Understanding Jesus as Savior: The promise of a Savior is a theme that runs throughout the Bible. This book will explore how Jesus fulfills the prophecies and promises made in Genesis, providing a comprehensive understanding of His role as the Redeemer of humanity.

4. Exploring the "I Am" Statements: Jesus' "I Am" statements in the New Testament are profound declarations of His divinity. By examining these statements in the context of God's self-revelation in the Old Testament, particularly the book of Genesis, we gain a deeper appreciation of Jesus' divine identity.

5. Encouraging Deeper Faith: Ultimately, this book aims to strengthen the reader's faith by providing a richer, more nuanced understanding of Jesus' nature and His place in God's eternal plan. By seeing the consistent message of salvation and divine love from Genesis to Revelation, readers will be encouraged to grow in their relationship with Jesus.

Structure

The book is organized into twelve chapters, each focusing on different aspects of Jesus' divinity and His connection to the book of Genesis. Here is a brief overview of the structure:

1. Introduction to the Divine Nature of Jesus: This chapter introduces the purpose and structure of the book, laying the groundwork for the exploration of Jesus' divinity and His connection to Genesis.

2. The Pre-Existence of Jesus: This chapter discusses the concept of Jesus' existence before His earthly life, supported by biblical references from both the Old and New Testaments.

3. Jesus in Creation: Here, we explore Jesus' role in the creation of the world and how Genesis hints at His involvement through the concept of the Trinity.

4. Jesus as the Promised Savior: This chapter examines the first prophecy of the Savior in Genesis 3:15 and how it is fulfilled in Jesus.

5. The "I Am" Statements of Jesus: We delve into the significance of Jesus' "I Am" statements and their connection to God's self-revelation in the Old Testament.

6. Jesus as the Seed of Abraham: This chapter highlights the promise made to Abraham and its fulfillment in Jesus, showing Jesus as the ultimate blessing to all nations.

7. The Sacrifice of Isaac and Jesus: We explore the parallels between the near-sacrifice of Isaac and Jesus' crucifixion, illustrating the concept of substitutionary atonement.

8. Jacob's Ladder and Jesus: This chapter examines Jacob's dream of a ladder reaching to heaven and its fulfillment in Jesus as the bridge between heaven and earth.

9. Joseph as a Type of Christ: We compare the story of Joseph with the life of Jesus, highlighting the similarities and foreshadowing of Jesus' redemptive work.

10. Jesus as the Fulfillment of the Law: This chapter discusses how Jesus fulfills the law and covenant established in Genesis and throughout the Old Testament.

11. Jesus and the New Creation: We explore the promise of a new creation, its roots in Genesis, and Jesus' role in bringing about this new reality.

12. Conclusion: The final chapter summarizes the key points discussed in the book, emphasizing the significance of understanding Jesus' divinity and His connection to Genesis.

Appendices and Bibliography

The book also includes several appendices and a comprehensive bibliography to provide additional resources and support for further study:

- Appendix A: Key Biblical Passages Referenced – A compilation of the essential Bible verses cited throughout the book for quick reference.

- Appendix B: Glossary of Theological Terms – Definitions of key terms used in the book to aid in understanding.

- Appendix C: Further Reading and Study Questions – Recommendations for further reading and questions for personal or group study to deepen engagement with the material.

- Bibliography: A list of sources and further reading materials on the divinity of Jesus and His connection to the Old Testament.

By structuring the book in this way, we aim to provide a comprehensive and accessible resource for understanding the divine nature of Jesus and His integral connection to the foundational truths of Genesis. Through careful study and reflection, readers will be equipped to appreciate the depth and richness of the biblical narrative and the central role of Jesus within it.

Jesus as "I Am"

Introduction to the Divine Nature of Jesus

In the journey to understand the divine nature of Jesus, one of the most profound and enlightening aspects is

His identification with the term "I Am." This self-designation not only reveals His divine identity but also connects Him directly with God's self-revelation in the Old Testament. This chapter aims to explore the significance of Jesus' "I Am" statements, their roots in the Old Testament, and their implications for our understanding of His divinity.

The Old Testament Foundation

The term "I Am" (Hebrew: אֶהְיֶה, Ehyeh) is first encountered in the book of Exodus, when God reveals Himself to Moses at the burning bush. In Exodus 3:13-14, Moses asks God what name he should give to the Israelites to authenticate his mission. God responds, "I AM WHO I AM." He said further, "Thus you shall say to the Israelites, 'I AM has sent me to you.'"

This declaration is significant for several reasons:

1. Self-Existence: The name "I Am" indicates God's self-existence and eternal presence. He is not dependent on anything or anyone for His existence.

2. Eternality: "I Am" signifies that God is eternal, existing beyond time and space.

3. Immutability: The name reflects God's unchanging nature. He is the same yesterday, today, and forever.

This foundational understanding sets the stage for the New Testament revelations of Jesus as "I Am."

Jesus' "I Am" Statements in the Gospel of John

The Gospel of John is particularly rich with Jesus' "I Am" statements, each revealing a different aspect of His divine identity and mission. These statements are direct assertions of His divinity, echoing God's self-revelation to Moses. Let's examine some of these profound declarations:

1. "I am the bread of life" (John 6:35, 48, 51): Jesus identifies Himself as the essential sustenance for spiritual life. Just as bread is necessary for physical survival, Jesus is necessary for spiritual sustenance and eternal life.

2. "I am the light of the world" (John 8:12): Jesus declares that He is the source of spiritual illumination. In a world darkened by sin, He brings the light of truth and life.

3. "I am the door of the sheep" (John 10:7, 9): Jesus presents Himself as the entry point to salvation. Through Him, believers gain access to God's kingdom and protection.

4. "I am the good shepherd" (John 10:11, 14): Jesus emphasizes His role as the caring and sacrificial leader of His followers. He knows His sheep and lays down His life for them.

5. "I am the resurrection and the life" (John 11:25): Jesus proclaims His power over life and death. He offers eternal life to all who believe in Him, conquering death through His resurrection.

6. "I am the way, and the truth, and the life" (John 14:6): Jesus declares that He is the exclusive path to God, embodying truth and the source of all life.

7. "I am the true vine" (John 15:1, 5): Jesus illustrates the vital relationship between Himself and His followers. As branches are dependent on the vine for sustenance, believers must remain connected to Jesus to bear spiritual fruit.

The Ultimate "I Am" Declaration

Perhaps the most striking "I Am" statement is found in John 8:58. During a confrontation with the Pharisees, Jesus says, "Truly, truly, I say to you, before Abraham was, I am." This statement is significant for several reasons:

1. Pre-Existence: Jesus asserts His existence before Abraham, who lived centuries before. This claim of pre-existence is a direct assertion of His divinity.

2. Equality with God: By using the phrase "I am," Jesus directly associates Himself with the God of Exodus 3:14. This declaration was understood by His audience as a claim to deity, which is why they attempted to stone Him for blasphemy (John 8:59).

Theological Implications of Jesus as "I Am"

1. Divine Identity: Jesus' "I Am" statements unequivocally affirm His divine nature. He is not just a prophet or teacher but God incarnate.

2. Mediator of God's Presence: Jesus as "I Am" bridges the gap between humanity and God. Through Him, we experience God's presence, truth, and life.

3. Source of Eternal Life: Jesus' identity as "I Am" underscores His role as the source of eternal life and salvation. Belief in Him is essential for reconciliation with God and eternal life.

4. Revelation of God's Character: Each "I Am" statement reveals different facets of God's character – His provision, guidance, protection, and truth.

Conclusion

Understanding Jesus as "I Am" enriches our comprehension of His divinity and mission. It connects the New Testament revelations with the Old Testament foundations, providing a coherent and profound picture of God's plan for salvation. Jesus is the eternal, self-existent God who came to dwell among us, offering light, life, and truth. As we delve deeper into the significance of these statements, we are invited to experience the fullness of who Jesus is and to place our trust in Him as our Lord and Savior.

The Relationship Between Jesus and the Old Testament, Particularly Genesis

Understanding the relationship between Jesus and the Old Testament is fundamental to grasping the fullness of His divinity and mission. The book of Genesis, as the first book of the Bible, lays the foundation for the entire biblical narrative and is deeply intertwined with the identity and work of Jesus. This chapter will explore how Genesis prefigures and points to Jesus, highlighting key themes and events that foreshadow His coming and mission.

Jesus in Creation

The opening verses of Genesis introduce us to the act of creation, where God speaks the universe into existence. In Genesis 1:1-3, we read, "In the beginning, God created the heavens and the earth... And God said, 'Let there be light,' and there was light." The New Testament reveals that Jesus, the Word, was instrumental in creation. John 1:1-3 states, "In the beginning was the Word, and the Word was with God, and the Word was God. He was with God in the beginning. Through Him all things were made; without Him nothing was made that has been made."

This passage from John's Gospel affirms that Jesus is the divine Logos (Word) through whom God created everything. Thus, Genesis and John together highlight Jesus' active role in creation, emphasizing His pre-existence and divinity.

The Promise of Redemption

Genesis 3:15 contains the first hint of the gospel message. After the fall of Adam and Eve, God addresses the serpent with a promise of redemption: "And I will put enmity between you and the woman, and between your offspring and hers; he will crush your head, and you will strike his heel." This verse, known as the Protoevangelium (the first gospel), foreshadows the ultimate victory of Jesus over Satan. Jesus, born of a woman, would defeat the powers of sin and death through His death and resurrection, crushing the serpent's head.

The Seed of Abraham

God's covenant with Abraham is another pivotal moment in Genesis that points to Jesus. In Genesis 12:3, God promises Abraham, "All peoples on earth will be blessed through you." Paul, in his letter to the Galatians, explains that this promise is fulfilled in Jesus Christ. Galatians 3:16 states, "The promises were spoken to Abraham and to his seed. Scripture does not say 'and to seeds,' meaning many people, but 'and to your seed,' meaning one person, who is Christ."

Jesus is the fulfillment of the covenant promises made to Abraham. He is the one through whom all nations are blessed, bringing salvation to the entire world.

The Sacrifice of Isaac

The story of Abraham and Isaac in Genesis 22 prefigures the sacrificial death of Jesus. God commands Abraham to offer his beloved son Isaac as a sacrifice. At the last moment, God provides a ram as a substitute, sparing Isaac's life. This event foreshadows the sacrifice of Jesus, God's only Son, who would be offered up for the sins of humanity. Unlike Isaac, Jesus was not spared; He became the sacrificial Lamb, taking on the sins of the world.

John the Baptist recognized Jesus as the fulfillment of this typology when he declared, "Behold, the Lamb of God, who takes away the sin of the world!" (John 1:29).

Jacob's Ladder

In Genesis 28:12, Jacob dreams of a ladder reaching from earth to heaven, with angels ascending and descending on it. Jesus alludes to this dream in John 1:51, saying, "Very truly I tell you, you will see heaven open, and the angels of God ascending and descending on the Son of Man." Jesus presents Himself as the true ladder, the bridge between heaven and earth. Through Him, the connection between God and humanity is restored, fulfilling the vision given to Jacob.

Joseph as a Type of Christ

The life of Joseph, recorded in Genesis 37-50, contains striking parallels to the life of Jesus. Joseph is betrayed by his brothers, sold into slavery, and suffers unjustly before being exalted to a position of power where he can save his family and others from famine. Similarly, Jesus is betrayed by His own people, suffers unjustly, and through His death and resurrection, brings salvation to humanity.

Joseph's forgiveness and provision for his brothers who wronged him foreshadow Jesus' forgiveness and grace extended to sinners. Joseph's story is a powerful typology of Jesus' redemptive work.

The Messianic Line

Genesis also establishes the lineage through which the Messiah would come. The genealogies and stories of the patriarchs (Abraham, Isaac, Jacob, and Judah) trace the lineage that leads to David and ultimately to Jesus. Genesis 49:10 contains a prophecy about Judah, saying, "The scepter will not depart from Judah, nor the ruler's staff from between his feet, until he to whom it belongs shall come and the obedience of the nations shall be his."

This prophecy points to Jesus, the Lion of the tribe of Judah, who would reign as King and command the obedience of the nations. The genealogical records in the Gospels of Matthew and Luke trace Jesus' ancestry back to these patriarchs, affirming His rightful place in this Messianic line.

Conclusion

The book of Genesis lays the groundwork for the entire biblical narrative, pointing forward to Jesus in numerous ways. From creation, the promise of redemption, and the covenant with Abraham, to the typologies of Isaac and Joseph, and the prophetic lineage, Genesis is replete with foreshadowings of Jesus' divine mission. Understanding these connections enriches our comprehension of Jesus as the fulfillment of God's promises and His integral role in the biblical story. Through these revelations, we see that Jesus is not an afterthought but the central figure of God's plan from the very beginning, the divine "I Am" who is intricately woven into the fabric of the Old Testament.

CHAPTER 02

THE PRE-EXISTENCE OF JESUS

The concept of Jesus' pre-existence is central to Christian theology, underscoring His divinity and eternal nature. Before Jesus' incarnation as a human being, He existed eternally with God the Father and the Holy Spirit. This chapter will explore the biblical foundations for Jesus' pre-existence, its theological significance, and its implications for understanding His identity and mission.

Biblical Foundations of Jesus' Pre-Existence

Several passages in the New Testament affirm the pre-existence of Jesus, revealing that He was active and present before His birth in Bethlehem. These scriptures highlight His divine nature and eternal relationship with God the Father.

1. John 1:1-3: "In the beginning was the Word, and the Word was with God, and the Word was God. He was with God in the beginning. Through Him all things were made; without Him nothing was made that has been made."

This passage unequivocally states that Jesus, referred to as the Word (Logos), existed from the beginning. He was with God and was God, playing an active role in creation.

2. Colossians 1:15-17: "The Son is the image of the invisible God, the firstborn over all creation. For in Him, all things were created: things in heaven and on earth, visible and invisible, whether thrones or powers or rulers or authorities; all things have been created through Him and for Him. He is before all things, and in Him all things hold together."

Paul's letter to the Colossians reinforces the idea of Jesus' pre-existence and His supremacy over all creation. As the agent of creation, Jesus existed before all things and sustains all things.

3. Hebrews 1:2-3: "But in these last days he has spoken to us by his Son, whom he appointed heir of all things, and through whom also he made the universe. The Son is the radiance of God's glory and the exact representation of his being, sustaining all things by his powerful word."

The author of Hebrews highlights that God created the universe through Jesus, who is the exact representation of God's being. This passage underscores Jesus' divine nature and pre-existence.

4. Philippians 2:6-7: "Who, being in very nature God, did not consider equality with God something to be used to his own advantage; rather, he made himself nothing by taking the very nature of a servant, being made in human likeness."

Paul explains that Jesus, although in very nature God, chose to humble Himself and take on human form. This passage indicates that Jesus existed in the form of God before His incarnation.

Theological Significance of Jesus' Pre-Existence

The pre-existence of Jesus is a profound theological truth that has several significant implications for understanding His identity and mission.

1. Affirmation of Divinity: Jesus' pre-existence affirms His divine nature. Unlike created beings, Jesus exists eternally, without beginning or end. This underscores His equality with God the Father and the Holy Spirit.

2. Eternal Sonship: Jesus' pre-existence highlights His eternal relationship with God the Father. He is the eternal Son, co-equal and co-eternal with the Father. This eternal sonship is foundational to the doctrine of the Trinity.

3. Role in Creation: The pre-existence of Jesus reveals His active role in creation. As the divine Logos, Jesus was the agent through whom all things were made. This establishes

His authority over creation and His ongoing involvement in sustaining it.

4. Foundation for Incarnation: The doctrine of Jesus' pre-existence is essential for understanding the incarnation. Jesus, the eternal Son of God, chose to take on human flesh and enter into human history. This voluntary act of humility and love is central to the Christian understanding of salvation.

Old Testament Foreshadowings

While the New Testament provides explicit affirmations of Jesus' pre-existence, the Old Testament contains foreshadowings and hints of His eternal nature.

1. Wisdom Literature: In Proverbs 8, wisdom is personified and described as existing before creation. Early Christians often interpreted this passage as a foreshadowing of Christ, who is the wisdom of God. Proverbs 8:22-23 states, "The Lord brought me forth as the first of his works, before his deeds of old; I was formed long ages ago, at the very beginning, when the world came to be."

2. The Angel of the Lord: Several Old Testament passages describe encounters with the Angel of the Lord, who speaks with divine authority and is often identified with God Himself. Many theologians see these appearances as pre-incarnate manifestations of Christ. For example, in Exodus 3:2-6, the Angel of the Lord appears to Moses in the burning

bush and declares, "I am the God of your father, the God of Abraham, the God of Isaac and the God of Jacob."

3. Theophanies: Various theophanies, or appearances of God in the Old Testament, are seen as pre-incarnate appearances of Christ. One notable example is in Genesis 18, where three visitors appear to Abraham, and one of them is identified as the Lord.

Implications for Christian Faith

Understanding the pre-existence of Jesus has profound implications for Christian faith and worship.

1. Worship and Adoration: Recognizing Jesus as the eternal Son of God who existed before all things enhances the depth of worship and adoration. Christians are called to worship Jesus not only as Savior but as the eternal, divine Creator.

2. Christ's Authority: Acknowledging Jesus' pre-existence reinforces His authority over all creation. As the one through whom all things were made, He has supreme authority and sovereignty, deserving of obedience and reverence.

3. Foundation for Salvation: The pre-existence of Jesus provides a foundation for understanding the magnitude of His incarnation and sacrifice. The eternal Son of God humbled Himself to become human and suffer for humanity's

redemption. This profound act of love is central to the Christian message of salvation.

4. Hope and Assurance: Belief in Jesus' pre-existence provides hope and assurance to believers. As the eternal, unchanging God, Jesus is a sure foundation for faith, providing stability and confidence in an ever-changing world.

Conclusion

The pre-existence of Jesus is a cornerstone of Christian theology, affirming His divinity, eternal nature, and active role in creation. This doctrine enriches our understanding of His incarnation, mission, and ongoing work in the world. By exploring the biblical foundations and theological implications of Jesus' pre-existence, we gain a deeper appreciation for the eternal Son of God who entered human history to bring salvation. As we continue to study the Scriptures, let us be continually awed by the mystery and majesty of Jesus, the pre-existent Word who became flesh and dwelt among us.

The Pre-Existence of Jesus

The concept of Jesus' pre-existence is foundational to understanding His divinity and eternal nature. Two critical New Testament passages that affirm this doctrine are John 1:1-3 and Colossians 1:15-17. This chapter will provide an expository study and comprehensive commentary on these passages, incorporating insights from exhaustive Strong's Concordance to delve deeper into the meaning and implications of Jesus' pre-existence.

Jesus' Pre-Existence According to John 1:1-3

John 1:1-3 (NIV):

1. In the beginning was the Word, and the Word was with God, and the Word was God.

2. He was with God in the beginning.

3. Through Him all things were made; without Him nothing was made that has been made.

Expository Study and Commentary

1. Verse 1: "In the beginning was the Word, and the Word was with God, and the Word was God."

- In the beginning: The phrase "in the beginning" (Greek: ἐν ἀρχῇ, Strong's G746) echoes Genesis 1:1, emphasizing that the Word (Jesus) existed at the very start of everything.

- The Word: The term "Word" (Greek: λόγος, Strong's G3056) refers to Jesus. In Greek philosophy and Jewish thought, Logos conveyed the idea of divine reason and creative order.

- With God: The phrase "was with God" (Greek: πρὸς τὸν θεόν, Strong's G4314) indicates a close, personal relationship. Jesus (the Word) existed in intimate communion with God the Father.

- Was God: The declaration "the Word was God" (Greek: καὶ θεὸς ἦν ὁ λόγος, Strong's G2316) unequivocally states that Jesus is divine. He shares the same essence and nature as God the Father.

2. Verse 2: "He was with God in the beginning."

- He was with God: Reiterating verse 1, this emphasizes the eternal coexistence of Jesus with God the Father.

- In the beginning: Reemphasizes Jesus' existence before creation, establishing His eternal nature.

3. Verse 3: "Through Him all things were made; without Him nothing was made that has been made."

- Through Him: Indicates that Jesus (the Word) was the agent of creation. All things were created through His divine power and authority.

- All things were made: The phrase "all things" (Greek: πάντα, Strong's G3956) signifies the totality of creation—everything that exists.

- Without Him nothing was made: Affirms that not a single thing came into existence apart from Jesus' creative work.

Strong's Concordance Insights

- Word (λόγος, Strong's G3056): In addition to "word," Logos can mean "reason," "speech," or "principle." In John's prologue, it signifies Jesus as the divine reason and communication of God.

- With (πρὸς, Strong's G4314): Often translated as "toward" or "with," this preposition indicates relational closeness and face-to-face presence.

- God (θεὸς, Strong's G2316): Used in both "the Word was with God" and "the Word was God," this term unequivocally denotes divinity.

Jesus' Pre-Existence According to Colossians 1:15-17

Colossians 1:15-17 (NIV):

15. The Son is the image of the invisible God, the firstborn over all creation.

16. For in Him all things were created: things in heaven and on earth, visible and invisible, whether thrones or powers or rulers or authorities; all things have been created through Him and for Him.

17. He is before all things, and in Him all things hold together.

Expository Study and Commentary

1. Verse 15: "The Son is the image of the invisible God, the firstborn over all creation."

- Image of the invisible God: The word "image" (Greek: εἰκών, Strong's G1504) means exact representation or likeness. Jesus perfectly represents and reveals the nature of the invisible God.

- Firstborn over all creation: The term "firstborn" (Greek: πρωτότοκος, Strong's G4416) denotes preeminence and priority in rank, not temporal sequence. Jesus is supreme over all creation, holding the highest position.

2. Verse 16: "For in Him all things were created: things in heaven and on earth, visible and invisible, whether thrones or powers or rulers or authorities; all things have been created through Him and for Him."

- In Him all things were created: Jesus is the sphere and means of creation. The phrase "in Him" (Greek: ἐν αὐτῷ, Strong's G1722 and G846) signifies His active role in the creation process.

- Things in heaven and on earth: This encompasses all realms of existence, emphasizing the comprehensiveness of Jesus' creative work.

- Visible and invisible: Indicates both the physical and spiritual dimensions of creation.

- Thrones, powers, rulers, authorities: Refers to various ranks of angels and spiritual beings, highlighting Jesus' authority over all.

- Through Him and for Him: All creation finds its source and purpose in Jesus.

3. Verse 17: "He is before all things, and in Him all things hold together."

- Before all things: Asserts Jesus' pre-existence and priority over creation.

- In Him all things hold together: Jesus sustains the universe. The phrase "hold together" (Greek: συνέστηκεν, Strong's G4921) implies that Jesus is the cohesive force maintaining order in creation.

Strong's Concordance Insights

- Image (εἰκών, Strong's G1504): Beyond physical likeness, it implies manifestation of inner essence and nature. Jesus manifests the very nature of God.

- Firstborn (πρωτότοκος, Strong's G4416): While it can denote birth order, here it emphasizes rank and preeminence. Jesus is the foremost and supreme over all creation.

- Hold together (συνέστηκεν, Strong's G4921): Means to cohere or sustain. Jesus is the one who keeps the universe orderly and functional.

Theological Implications

1. Affirmation of Divinity: Both passages unequivocally affirm Jesus' divine nature. He is not a created

being but the eternal Son of God, fully divine and co-equal with God the Father.

2. Role in Creation: Jesus' active role in creation underscores His authority and power. All things were made through Him, for Him, and He sustains everything.

3. Revelation of God: Jesus is the perfect revelation of God's nature. In seeing Jesus, we see God. His life and works reflect the character and essence of the invisible God.

Conclusion

The pre-existence of Jesus is a cornerstone of Christian faith, underscoring His eternal divinity and integral role in creation. John 1:1-3 and Colossians 1:15-17 provide profound insights into this truth, revealing Jesus as the eternal Word and the image of the invisible God. Through a careful expository study and examination of these passages, enriched by insights from Strong's Concordance, we gain a deeper understanding of the majesty and mystery of Jesus Christ. He is the eternal Son, through whom and for whom all things were created, and in whom all things hold together.

Jesus in Genesis 1:1 – The Eternal Nature of God and Jesus

The opening verse of the Bible, Genesis 1:1, states, "In the beginning God created the heavens and the earth." This foundational declaration sets the stage for the entire biblical narrative, affirming the existence of an eternal, sovereign Creator. This chapter explores how Jesus is intrinsically linked to this verse, emphasizing His eternal nature and role in creation. By examining the plural noun Elohim and other relevant biblical passages, we will reveal Jesus as a central figure in the act of creation.

Genesis 1:1 and the Eternal Nature of God

Genesis 1:1 (NIV): "In the beginning God created the heavens and the earth."

- In the beginning: This phrase (Hebrew: בְּרֵאשִׁית, Bereshit) marks the commencement of time and the universe. It signifies the starting point of creation but not the beginning of God, who exists eternally.

- God: The term used here is Elohim (אֱלֹהִים, Strong's H430), a plural noun that conveys the majesty and power of the Creator. The use of Elohim suggests a complex unity within the Godhead.

Jesus as Part of Genesis 1:1

The New Testament provides deeper insights into Jesus' involvement in creation, affirming His eternal existence and divine role. John 1:1-3 and Colossians 1:15-17 are key passages that connect Jesus directly to Genesis 1:1.

John 1:1-3 (NIV):

1. In the beginning was the Word, and the Word was with God, and the Word was God.

2. He was with God in the beginning.

3. Through Him all things were made; without Him nothing was made that has been made.

- In the beginning: John's Gospel echoes Genesis 1:1, indicating that Jesus (the Word) was present at the start of creation.

- The Word was with God: This phrase highlights the intimate relationship between Jesus and God the Father.

- The Word was God: Affirming the divinity of Jesus, John declares that Jesus is fully God.

- Through Him all things were made: This confirms Jesus' active role in creation, establishing Him as the agent through whom God created everything.

Colossians 1:15-17 (NIV):

15. The Son is the image of the invisible God, the firstborn over all creation.

16. For in Him all things were created: things in heaven and on earth, visible and invisible, whether thrones or powers or rulers or authorities; all things have been created through Him and for Him.

17. He is before all things, and in Him all things hold together.

- Image of the invisible God: Jesus perfectly represents and reveals God.

- Firstborn over all creation: Jesus is preeminent and supreme over all creation.

- In Him all things were created: Jesus is the sphere and means of creation.

- Through Him and for Him: Creation exists through and for Jesus, affirming His central role in God's creative work.

- He is before all things: Jesus existed before anything else, underscoring His eternal nature.

- In Him all things hold together: Jesus sustains the universe, maintaining its order and coherence.

The Plural Noun Elohim

The use of the plural noun Elohim in Genesis 1:1 is significant. Although it is a plural form, it is consistently used with singular verbs and adjectives when referring to the one true God, indicating a complex unity.

1. Genesis 1:26: "Then God said, 'Let us make mankind in our image, in our likeness...'"

- The plural pronouns "us" and "our" suggest a divine council or plurality within the Godhead. This plurality is understood in Christian theology as the Trinity: Father, Son, and Holy Spirit.

2. Genesis 3:22: "And the Lord God said, 'The man has now become like one of us, knowing good and evil.'"

- Again, the plural pronoun "us" indicates a conversation within the Godhead, affirming the presence of multiple persons within the unity of God.

3. Isaiah 6:8: "Then I heard the voice of the Lord saying, 'Whom shall I send? And who will go for us?'"

- This verse reinforces the concept of plurality within the singularity of God, further supporting the idea of the Trinity.

Expository Insights from Strong's Concordance

- Elohim (אֱלֹהִים, Strong's H430): Elohim is a plural noun used over 2,500 times in the Old Testament. While it can refer to gods or divine beings, when referring to the God of Israel, it denotes a singular entity with a plurality of persons, indicating the Trinity.

- Created (בָּרָא, bara, Strong's H1254): This verb is used exclusively with God as the subject, emphasizing that creation is a divine act. The use of Elohim with bara underscores the singular action of the plural God.

Jesus as Part of Elohim

The New Testament affirms that Jesus is part of the divine Elohim, participating fully in the unity and plurality of the Godhead.

John 17:5 (NIV): "And now, Father, glorify me in your presence with the glory I had with you before the world began."

- Jesus speaks of the glory He shared with the Father before creation, affirming His pre-existence and divinity.

Hebrews 1:2-3 (NIV): "But in these last days he has spoken to us by his Son, whom he appointed heir of all things, and through whom also he made the universe. The Son is the radiance of God's glory and the exact representation of his being, sustaining all things by his powerful word."

- This passage reiterates that Jesus is the agent of creation, the exact representation of God, and the sustainer of the universe.

Philippians 2:6-7 (NIV): "Who, being in very nature God, did not consider equality with God something to be used to his own advantage; rather, he made himself nothing by taking the very nature of a servant, being made in human likeness."

- Paul's description of Jesus as being in very nature God underscores His equality with God and His pre-existence.

Theological Implications

1. Unity in Diversity: The use of Elohim and the New Testament affirmations of Jesus' role in creation highlight the unity and diversity within the Godhead. The Father, Son, and Holy Spirit work together in perfect harmony, each fully participating in the divine essence.

2. Jesus' Divine Authority: As part of Elohim, Jesus possesses full divine authority. His words and actions carry the weight of divine power and purpose.

3. Foundation for Salvation: Understanding Jesus' role in creation and His pre-existence underscores the significance of His incarnation and atoning work. The eternal Creator entered His creation to redeem and restore it.

Conclusion

Genesis 1:1, with its declaration of God's creative work, serves as a foundational text for understanding the eternal nature and divine role of Jesus. The New Testament passages in John 1:1-3 and Colossians 1:15-17, along with the use of the plural noun Elohim, reveal Jesus as the eternal Word and the divine agent of creation. These connections underscore the unity and complexity of the Godhead, highlighting Jesus' pre-existence, divinity, and central role in God's plan for the universe. By recognizing Jesus as part of Elohim, we gain a deeper appreciation of His majesty and the profound mystery of the Trinity.

CHAPTER 03

JESUS IN CREATION

Understanding Jesus' role in creation is fundamental to grasping His divinity and the breadth of His mission. The New Testament sheds light on Jesus as the divine agent through whom all things were made. This chapter will explore Jesus' integral role in creation, focusing on Colossians 1:16 and 1 Corinthians 8:6. Through expository study and comprehensive commentary, enriched by insights from Strong's Concordance, we will delve into the profound implications of Jesus' creative work.

Colossians 1:16 and Jesus' Role in Creation

Colossians 1:16 (NIV): "For in Him all things were created: things in heaven and on earth, visible and invisible, whether thrones or powers or rulers or authorities; all things have been created through Him and for Him."

Expository Study and Commentary

- For in Him all things were created: The phrase "in Him" (Greek: ἐν αὐτῷ, Strong's G1722 and G846) indicates that Jesus is the sphere within which creation occurs. All things exist within His sovereign domain and by His creative power.

- Things in heaven and on earth: This expression encompasses the entirety of creation, both the physical and spiritual realms.

- Visible and invisible: This indicates that Jesus' creative work includes everything from the material universe to the spiritual beings.

- Thrones, powers, rulers, authorities: Refers to various hierarchies of angelic beings and spiritual powers. Jesus is the creator of all such entities, underscoring His supremacy over the spiritual realm.

- All things have been created through Him and for Him: This highlights Jesus as both the means and the goal of creation. Creation comes into existence through His power and exists for His glory and purposes.

Strong's Concordance Insights

- In (ἐν, Strong's G1722): Denotes the sphere or realm in which action takes place, signifying Jesus as the environment of creation.

- Him (αὐτός, Strong's G846): Refers to Jesus, emphasizing His centrality in the creation process.

- Created (κτίζω, Strong's G2936): Means to create or form, used exclusively in relation to divine creation.

- Through (διά, Strong's G1223): Indicates the means or instrumentality, affirming Jesus as the agent through whom creation occurs.

- For (εἰς, Strong's G1519): Signifies purpose or direction, highlighting that all creation exists for Jesus' purposes and glory.

1 Corinthians 8:6 and Jesus' Role in Creation

1 Corinthians 8:6 (NIV): "Yet for us there is but one God, the Father, from whom all things came and for whom we live; and there is but one Lord, Jesus Christ, through whom all things came and through whom we live."

Expository Study and Commentary

- One God, the Father, from whom all things came and for whom we live: Acknowledges God the Father as the ultimate source of all things, emphasizing the monotheistic belief in one God.

- One Lord, Jesus Christ: Declares Jesus as the one Lord, affirming His divine status and authority.

- Through whom all things came: Indicates that Jesus is the agent of creation, through whom the Father brings everything into existence.

- Through whom we live: Jesus is not only the agent of creation but also the sustainer of life. Believers live through Him, relying on His ongoing provision and sustenance.

Strong's Concordance Insights

- Through (διά, Strong's G1223): Same as in Colossians 1:16, emphasizing Jesus as the instrumental means of creation.

- All things (πάντα, Strong's G3956): Refers to the entirety of creation, both material and spiritual.

- Live (ζάω, Strong's G2198): Means to live or be alive, indicating that our existence and sustenance depend on Jesus.

Theological Implications of Jesus' Role in Creation

1. Divine Authority: Jesus' role in creation affirms His divine authority. As the agent through whom all things were made, He possesses supreme power over the universe.

2. Purpose of Creation: Creation exists for Jesus. All things were made by Him and for Him, meaning that the ultimate purpose of creation is to glorify and serve Him.

3. Sustainer of Life: Jesus is not only the creator but also the sustainer. Our ongoing existence and the coherence of the universe depend on His continuous upholding.

4. Unity with the Father: Jesus' role in creation highlights His unity with the Father. While the Father is the source, Jesus is the means, demonstrating the harmonious working of the Trinity in creation.

The Plurality of Elohim and Jesus in Creation

As discussed in the previous chapter, the use of the plural noun Elohim in Genesis 1:1 suggests a complex unity within the Godhead. This plurality is further revealed in the New Testament, where Jesus is identified as the divine agent of creation, working in perfect unity with the Father.

1. Genesis 1:26: "Then God said, 'Let us make mankind in our image, in our likeness...'"

- The plural pronouns "us" and "our" indicate a conversation within the Godhead, involving multiple persons. This plurality is understood as the Father, Son, and Holy Spirit working together in creation.

2. Isaiah 6:8: "Then I heard the voice of the Lord saying, 'Whom shall I send? And who will go for us?'"

- The use of "us" once again suggests a plurality within the unity of God, pointing to the triune nature of the Godhead.

John 17:5 (NIV): "And now, Father, glorify me in your presence with the glory I had with you before the world began."

- Jesus speaks of the glory He shared with the Father before creation, affirming His pre-existence and divine role.

Hebrews 1:2-3 (NIV): "But in these last days he has spoken to us by his Son, whom he appointed heir of all things, and through whom also he made the universe. The Son is the radiance of God's glory and the exact representation of his being, sustaining all things by his powerful word."

- This passage reiterates that Jesus is the agent of creation, the exact representation of God, and the sustainer of the universe.

Conclusion

The exploration of Jesus' role in creation, as revealed in Colossians 1:16 and 1 Corinthians 8:6, provides a profound understanding of His divine authority and eternal nature. Through expository study and comprehensive commentary, we see that Jesus is the divine agent through whom all things were made and for whom all things exist. The use of the plural noun Elohim in Genesis 1:1 further underscores the complex unity within the Godhead, highlighting Jesus' integral role in the act of creation. Understanding Jesus as the creator and sustainer enriches our faith, affirming His divinity and His central place in the divine plan for the universe.

The Plurality in Genesis 1:26 – "Let Us Make Man in Our Image"

Genesis 1:26 is a profound verse that offers a glimpse into the plurality within the Godhead, which Christian theology understands as the Trinity. The use of plural pronouns "us" and "our" in this verse suggests a complex unity involving multiple persons. This chapter will explore Genesis 1:26 in depth, examining its implications for understanding the Trinity and Jesus' role in creation. Through expository study and comprehensive commentary, enriched by insights from Strong's Concordance, we will delve into the significance of God's plural pronouns and their occurrences in other biblical references.

Genesis 1:26 – Expository Study and Commentary

Genesis 1:26 (NIV): "Then God said, 'Let us make mankind in our image, in our likeness, so that they may rule over the fish in the sea and the birds in the sky, over the livestock and all the wild animals, and over all the creatures that move along the ground.'"

Expository Study and Commentary

1. Then God said: The term "God" here is Elohim (אֱלֹהִים, Strong's H430), a plural noun used for the singular God of Israel. The use of Elohim suggests a complex unity within the Godhead.

2. Let us make: The phrase "let us make" (Hebrew: נַעֲשֶׂה, na'aseh, Strong's H6213) indicates a deliberative process

among multiple persons. This plural pronoun implies a conversation within the Godhead, hinting at the Trinity.

3. Man in our image, in our likeness: The plural pronouns "our" (Hebrew: צַלְמֵנוּ, tzalmenu, Strong's H6754) and "likeness" (Hebrew: דְּמוּתֵנוּ, demutenu, Strong's H1823) reinforce the idea of plurality within the divine nature. Humans are created to reflect the relational and communal aspects of God.

4. So that they may rule: The purpose of creating humans in God's image is to give them dominion over the earth. This reflects God's sovereign rule and the responsibility given to humanity.

Strong's Concordance Insights

- Elohim (אֱלֹהִים, Strong's H430): A plural noun used for God, suggesting a unity of multiple persons. It emphasizes the majesty and fullness of the divine nature.

- Make (עָשָׂה, asah, Strong's H6213): Means to create or fashion, indicating intentional and purposeful action.

- Image (צֶלֶם, tselem, Strong's H6754): Refers to a representation or likeness, indicating that humans are created to reflect God's nature.

- Likeness (דְּמוּת, demuth, Strong's H1823): Similarity or resemblance, emphasizing the attributes of God reflected in humanity.

The Plural Pronouns and the Trinity

The use of plural pronouns in Genesis 1:26 has long intrigued scholars and theologians. Christian doctrine interprets these pronouns as evidence of the Trinity – one God in three persons: Father, Son, and Holy Spirit.

1. Genesis 3:22: "And the Lord God said, 'The man has now become like one of us, knowing good and evil.'"

- The plural pronoun "us" indicates a conversation within the Godhead, similar to Genesis 1:26. It suggests a plurality of persons involved in the divine deliberation.

2. Genesis 11:7: "Come, let us go down and confuse their language so they will not understand each other."

- At the Tower of Babel, God speaks in the plural form, indicating a unified action taken by the Godhead.

3. Isaiah 6:8: "Then I heard the voice of the Lord saying, 'Whom shall I send? And who will go for us?'"

- In Isaiah's vision, God uses both singular and plural pronouns, reflecting the complex unity within the divine nature.

4. John 17:21-23: "That all of them may be one, Father, just as you are in me and I am in you. May they also be in us so that the world may believe that you have sent me."

- Jesus' prayer emphasizes the unity and relational aspect of the Godhead, inviting believers into this divine fellowship.

Trinitarian Implications

The plural pronouns in Genesis 1:26 and other passages underscore the relational nature of the Trinity. The Father, Son, and Holy Spirit exist in perfect unity and harmony, working together in creation and redemption. This plurality within unity is a foundational aspect of Christian theology, revealing the depth and mystery of God's nature.

Jesus' Role in the Trinity and Creation

The New Testament provides further clarity on Jesus' role within the Trinity, particularly in the act of creation.

John 1:1-3 (NIV):

1. In the beginning was the Word, and the Word was with God, and the Word was God.

2. He was with God in the beginning.

3. Through Him all things were made; without Him nothing was made that has been made.

- The Word (λόγος, logos, Strong's G3056): Refers to Jesus, who is both distinct from and fully God. He is the divine agent through whom all things were made.

- With God (πρὸς τὸν θεόν, pros ton theon, Strong's G4314 and G2316): Indicates an intimate relationship and equality with God the Father.

- All things were made (γίνομαι, ginomai, Strong's G1096): Affirms Jesus' role as the creator of everything.

Colossians 1:16 (NIV): "For in Him all things were created: things in heaven and on earth, visible and invisible, whether thrones or powers or rulers or authorities; all things have been created through Him and for Him."

- In Him (ἐν αὐτῷ, en auto, Strong's G1722 and G846): Signifies that Jesus is the realm and means of creation.

- Through Him (διά, dia, Strong's G1223): Affirms Jesus as the instrument through whom creation occurs.

- For Him (εἰς αὐτόν, eis auton, Strong's G1519 and G846): Indicates that all creation exists for Jesus' purposes and glory.

Theological Significance

1. Relational Nature of God: The plurality within the Godhead highlights the relational aspect of God's nature. Humanity, created in God's image, is designed for relationship with God and with one another.

2. Unity and Diversity: The Trinity exemplifies perfect unity and diversity. The Father, Son, and Holy Spirit are distinct persons yet fully one in essence and purpose.

3. Jesus' Divine Authority: As part of the Trinity, Jesus possesses full divine authority. His role in creation underscores His power and preeminence.

Conclusion

Genesis 1:26, with its use of plural pronouns "us" and "our," offers a profound insight into the complex unity of the Godhead, which Christian theology understands as the Trinity. This verse, along with other biblical references, reveals the relational and communal nature of God, involving the Father, Son, and Holy Spirit in the act of creation. The New Testament further illuminates Jesus' integral role within the Trinity, highlighting His divine authority and creative power. Understanding the plurality in Genesis 1:26 enriches our comprehension of the Trinity and the profound mystery of God's nature, inviting us into a deeper relationship with the triune God.

The Significance of Jesus as the Word Through Whom All Things Were Made

The New Testament provides profound insights into the role of Jesus in creation, especially through the passages of John 1:1-3 and Colossians 1:16. These verses highlight Jesus as the divine Word and the agent through whom all things were made. This chapter will explore the significance of Jesus as the Word, integrating the insights from John 1:1-3 and Colossians 1:16, using expository study and comprehensive commentary enriched by exhaustive Strong's Concordance analysis.

John 1:1-3 – Expository Study and Commentary

John 1:1-3 (NIV):

1. In the beginning was the Word, and the Word was with God, and the Word was God.

2. He was with God in the beginning.

3. Through Him all things were made; without Him nothing was made that has been made.

Verse 1: "In the beginning was the Word, and the Word was with God, and the Word was God."

- In the beginning: The phrase "in the beginning" (Greek: ἐν ἀρχῇ, Strong's G746) parallels Genesis 1:1, indicating the eternal nature of the Word (Jesus). It signifies that Jesus existed before the creation of the world.

- The Word: The term "Word" (Greek: λόγος, logos, Strong's G3056) refers to Jesus. In Greek philosophy and Jewish thought, Logos conveyed the idea of divine reason, order, and communication.

- Was with God: The phrase "was with God" (Greek: πρὸς τὸν θεόν, pros ton theon, Strong's G4314 and G2316) implies an intimate relationship between Jesus and God the Father, indicating distinct persons within the Godhead.

- Was God: The declaration "the Word was God" (Greek: καὶ θεὸς ἦν ὁ λόγος, kai theos en ho logos, Strong's G2316) affirms the full divinity of Jesus, sharing the same essence as God the Father.

Verse 2: "He was with God in the beginning."

- He was with God: This reiterates the pre-existence of Jesus and His eternal communion with God the Father. It emphasizes His distinct personhood within the Trinity.

- In the beginning: Reinforces that Jesus existed from eternity past, before the creation of the world.

Verse 3: "Through Him all things were made; without Him nothing was made that has been made."

- Through Him: Indicates that Jesus (the Word) was the agent of creation. The phrase "through Him" (Greek: δι' αὐτοῦ, dia autou, Strong's G1223 and G846) signifies His instrumental role in bringing everything into existence.

- All things were made: The phrase "all things" (Greek: πάντα, panta, Strong's G3956) encompasses the entirety of creation—everything that exists.

- Without Him nothing was made: Affirms that not a single thing came into existence apart from Jesus' creative work, underscoring His essential role in creation.

Strong's Concordance Insights

- Word (λόγος, logos, Strong's G3056): In addition to "word," Logos can mean "reason," "speech," or "principle." In John's prologue, it signifies Jesus as the divine reason and communication of God.

- With (πρὸς, pros, Strong's G4314): Often translated as "toward" or "with," this preposition indicates relational closeness and face-to-face presence.

- God (θεός, theos, Strong's G2316): Used in both "the Word was with God" and "the Word was God," this term unequivocally denotes divinity.

- Made (γίνομαι, ginomai, Strong's G1096): Means to become or come into being, emphasizing the act of creation.

Colossians 1:16 – Integral to John 1:1-3

Colossians 1:16 (NIV): "For in Him all things were created: things in heaven and on earth, visible and invisible, whether thrones or powers or rulers or authorities; all things have been created through Him and for Him."

Expository Study and Commentary

- In Him all things were created: The phrase "in Him" (Greek: ἐν αὐτῷ, en auto, Strong's G1722 and G846) indicates that Jesus is the sphere within which creation occurs. All things exist within His sovereign domain and by His creative power.

- Things in heaven and on earth: This expression encompasses the entirety of creation, both the physical and spiritual realms, emphasizing the comprehensive scope of Jesus' creative work.

- Visible and invisible: Indicates that Jesus' creative work includes everything from the material universe to spiritual beings.

- Thrones, powers, rulers, authorities: Refers to various hierarchies of angelic beings and spiritual powers. Jesus is the creator of all such entities, underscoring His supremacy over the spiritual realm.

- All things have been created through Him and for Him: This highlights Jesus as both the means and the goal of creation. Creation comes into existence through His power and exists for His glory and purposes.

Strong's Concordance Insights

- In (ἐν, en, Strong's G1722): Denotes the sphere or realm in which action takes place, signifying Jesus as the environment of creation.

- Him (αὐτός, autos, Strong's G846): Refers to Jesus, emphasizing His centrality in the creation process.

- Created (κτίζω, ktizo, Strong's G2936): Means to create or form, used exclusively in relation to divine creation.

- Through (διά, dia, Strong's G1223): Indicates the means or instrumentality, affirming Jesus as the agent through whom creation occurs.

- For (εἰς, eis, Strong's G1519): Signifies purpose or direction, highlighting that all creation exists for Jesus' purposes and glory.

Theological Implications

1. Divine Authority: Jesus' role in creation affirms His divine authority. As the agent through whom all things were made, He possesses supreme power over the universe.

2. Purpose of Creation: Creation exists for Jesus. All things were made by Him and for Him, meaning that the ultimate purpose of creation is to glorify and serve Him.

3. Sustainer of Life: Jesus is not only the creator but also the sustainer. Our ongoing existence and the coherence of the universe depend on His continuous upholding.

4. Unity with the Father: Jesus' role in creation highlights His unity with the Father. While the Father is the source, Jesus is the means, demonstrating the harmonious working of the Trinity in creation.

The Plurality in Genesis 1:26 and Jesus' Role

Genesis 1:26 (NIV): "Then God said, 'Let us make mankind in our image, in our likeness...'"

- Let us make: The phrase "let us make" (Hebrew: נַעֲשֶׂה, na'aseh, Strong's H6213) indicates a deliberative process among multiple persons. This plural pronoun implies a conversation within the Godhead, hinting at the Trinity.

- Our image, our likeness: The plural pronouns "our" (Hebrew: צַלְמֵנוּ, tzalmenu, Strong's H6754) and "likeness" (Hebrew: דְּמוּתֵנוּ, demutenu, Strong's H1823) reinforce the idea of plurality within the divine nature. Humans are created to reflect the relational and communal aspects of God.

Other Biblical References to Plural Pronouns for God

1. Genesis 3:22: "And the Lord God said, 'The man has now become like one of us, knowing good and evil.'"

2. Genesis 11:7: "Come, let us go down and confuse their language so they will not understand each other."

3. Isaiah 6:8: "Then I heard the voice of the Lord saying, 'Whom shall I send? And who will go for us?'"

These references highlight the relational and communal nature of the Godhead, involving multiple persons in divine deliberation and action.

Conclusion

The significance of Jesus as the Word through whom all things were made is profoundly illuminated in John 1:1-3 and Colossians 1:16. These passages reveal Jesus as the divine agent of creation, affirming His pre-existence, authority, and integral role within the Godhead. The use of plural pronouns in Genesis 1:26 and other biblical references further underscores the complex unity of the Trinity. Understanding Jesus' role in creation enriches our faith, highlighting His divine nature and the profound mystery of the triune God. All creation exists through and for Jesus, underscoring His central place in God's eternal plan.

CHAPTER 04

JESUS AS THE PROMISED SAVIOR

Genesis 3:15 is often referred to as the Protoevangelium, meaning the "first gospel." It is the first prophecy of a Savior in the Bible, offering a glimpse of God's redemptive plan immediately after the fall of humanity. This verse holds significant theological importance as it introduces the promise of Jesus Christ, the Messiah, who would ultimately defeat sin and Satan. This chapter will explore Genesis 3:15 in depth, examining its context, meaning, and fulfillment in Jesus Christ.

Genesis 3:15 – Expository Study and Commentary

Genesis 3:15 (NIV): "And I will put enmity between you and the woman, and between your offspring and hers; he will crush your head, and you will strike his heel."

Context of Genesis 3:15

After Adam and Eve's disobedience in the Garden of Eden, God pronounces judgment on the serpent (Satan), the woman, and the man. Genesis 3:15 is part of God's curse on the serpent, but it also contains a promise of redemption for humanity.

1. The Serpent (Satan): The serpent, used by Satan to deceive Eve, represents evil and opposition to God.

2. The Woman (Eve): Eve represents humanity, especially in her role as the mother of all living.

3. The Offspring: The "offspring" or "seed" (Hebrew: זֶרַע, zera, Strong's H2233) can be interpreted collectively (referring to humanity) and singularly (referring to a specific individual).

Verse Analysis

- "I will put enmity between you and the woman": God declares that there will be ongoing hostility between the serpent (Satan) and the woman (Eve) and their respective descendants. This enmity signifies the spiritual battle between good and evil.

- "And between your offspring and hers": The term "offspring" (Hebrew: זֶרַע, zera) refers to the descendants of both the serpent and the woman. While this includes all of humanity, it also points to a specific descendant of the woman who will play a pivotal role in this battle.

- "He will crush your head": The pronoun "he" (Hebrew: הוּא, hu, Strong's H1931) points to a singular, male offspring who will ultimately defeat the serpent. Crushing the head signifies a decisive and fatal blow, indicating ultimate victory.

- "And you will strike his heel": The serpent striking the heel of the woman's offspring suggests that the serpent will inflict harm but not a fatal blow. This wound signifies the suffering and temporary setback experienced by the promised Savior.

Strong's Concordance Insights

- Enmity (אֵיבָה, eybah, Strong's H342): Refers to hostility or animosity, emphasizing the ongoing conflict between Satan and humanity.

- Offspring (זֶרַע, zera, Strong's H2233): Means seed or descendants, used both collectively for all descendants and specifically for a particular individual.

- Crush (שׁוּף, shuph, Strong's H7779): Means to bruise or crush, indicating a decisive, forceful action.

- Strike (שׁוּף, shuph, Strong's H7779): The same Hebrew word is used for both "crush" and "strike," but the context differentiates the severity of the actions.

The Promise of the Savior in Genesis 3:15

The Protoevangelium: The First Gospel

Genesis 3:15 is recognized as the first announcement of the gospel. Despite the immediate judgment on humanity, God offers a promise of hope and redemption through a future Savior. This prophecy introduces several key themes that are central to the Christian understanding of salvation.

1. The Seed of the Woman: The prophecy points to a specific descendant of Eve who will defeat the serpent. This "seed" is identified in the New Testament as Jesus Christ.

2. The Battle Between Good and Evil: The enmity between the serpent and the woman's offspring symbolizes the spiritual battle that culminates in Christ's victory over sin and Satan.

3. The Ultimate Victory: The crushing of the serpent's head by the woman's offspring signifies the ultimate triumph of Jesus over Satan, sin, and death.

Fulfillment in Jesus Christ

The New Testament identifies Jesus as the fulfillment of the promise made in Genesis 3:15. Several passages highlight this connection and the realization of God's redemptive plan through Christ.

1. Galatians 4:4-5 (NIV): "But when the set time had fully come, God sent his Son, born of a woman, born under the law, to redeem those under the law, that we might receive adoption to sonship."

- Born of a woman: Paul emphasizes Jesus' humanity and His role as the promised seed of the woman.

- To redeem: Jesus' mission is to redeem humanity from the curse of sin, fulfilling the promise of Genesis 3:15.

2. Hebrews 2:14 (NIV): "Since the children have flesh and blood, he too shared in their humanity so that by his death he might break the power of him who holds the power of death—that is, the devil."

- Break the power of the devil: Jesus' death and resurrection defeat Satan, fulfilling the promise of crushing the serpent's head.

3. 1 John 3:8 (NIV): "The reason the Son of God appeared was to destroy the devil's work."

- Destroy the devil's work: Jesus' incarnation and victory over sin and death are the ultimate fulfillment of the Protoevangelium.

Theological Implications

1. God's Redemptive Plan: Genesis 3:15 reveals that God's plan for redemption was established immediately after the fall. It underscores God's sovereignty and His commitment to restoring humanity.

2. The Promise of a Savior: The prophecy points to Jesus as the Savior who would defeat sin and Satan. This early

promise sets the stage for the unfolding narrative of salvation throughout the Bible.

3. The Victory of Christ: The crushing of the serpent's head signifies the definitive victory of Jesus over the forces of evil. This victory is central to the Christian faith, offering hope and assurance of salvation.

Conclusion

Genesis 3:15, known as the Protoevangelium, is a foundational prophecy that introduces the promise of a Savior immediately after the fall of humanity. This verse foreshadows the coming of Jesus Christ, who would ultimately defeat sin and Satan through His death and resurrection. The New Testament affirms Jesus as the fulfillment of this promise, highlighting His role as the Redeemer and Victor over evil. Understanding Genesis 3:15 enriches our appreciation of God's redemptive plan and the centrality of Jesus in the biblical narrative. Through this prophecy, we see the profound hope and assurance that God offers to humanity, even in the midst of judgment.

The Protoevangelium and Its Fulfillment in Jesus

The Protoevangelium, or "first gospel," is a foundational prophecy found in Genesis 3:15. It marks the first mention of a Savior and the promise of redemption in the Bible. This chapter explores the Protoevangelium's context, significance, and fulfillment in Jesus Christ. By understanding this prophecy, we can better appreciate God's redemptive plan that unfolds throughout the Scriptures and culminates in the life, death, and resurrection of Jesus.

The Protoevangelium in Genesis 3:15

Genesis 3:15 (NIV): "And I will put enmity between you and the woman, and between your offspring and hers; he will crush your head, and you will strike his heel."

Context of the Protoevangelium

The Protoevangelium appears in the aftermath of the Fall, when Adam and Eve disobey God by eating from the Tree of the Knowledge of Good and Evil. This act of disobedience introduces sin and death into the world. In response, God pronounces judgments on the serpent, the woman, and the man. Genesis 3:15 is part of God's curse on the serpent, but it also contains a promise of hope and redemption for humanity.

1. The Serpent (Satan): The serpent, who deceived Eve, represents Satan and the forces of evil.

2. The Woman (Eve): Eve symbolizes humanity, especially in her role as the mother of all living.

3. The Offspring: The term "offspring" (Hebrew: זֶרַע, zera, Strong's H2233) refers to the descendants of both the serpent and the woman. It can be interpreted collectively (all

of humanity) and singularly (a specific individual who will deliver a decisive blow).

Verse Analysis

- "I will put enmity between you and the woman": God declares ongoing hostility between the serpent (Satan) and the woman (Eve) and their respective descendants. This enmity signifies the spiritual battle between good and evil.

- "And between your offspring and hers": The term "offspring" (Hebrew: זֶרַע, zera) refers to the descendants of both the serpent and the woman. While this includes all humanity, it also points to a specific descendant of the woman who will play a pivotal role in this battle.

- "He will crush your head": The pronoun "he" (Hebrew: הוּא, hu, Strong's H1931) indicates a singular, male offspring who will ultimately defeat the serpent. Crushing the head signifies a decisive and fatal blow, indicating ultimate victory.

- "And you will strike his heel": The serpent striking the heel of the woman's offspring suggests that the serpent will inflict harm but not a fatal blow. This wound signifies the suffering and temporary setback experienced by the promised Savior.

Strong's Concordance Insights

- Enmity (אֵיבָה, eybah, Strong's H342): Refers to hostility or animosity, emphasizing the ongoing conflict between Satan and humanity.

- Offspring (זֶרַע, zera, Strong's H2233): Means seed or descendants, used both collectively for all descendants and specifically for a particular individual.

- Crush (שׁוּף, shuph, Strong's H7779): Means to bruise or crush, indicating a decisive, forceful action.

- Strike (שׁוּף, shuph, Strong's H7779): The same Hebrew word is used for both "crush" and "strike," but the context differentiates the severity of the actions.

The Promise of the Savior in the Protoevangelium

The First Gospel

Genesis 3:15 is recognized as the first announcement of the gospel. Despite the immediate judgment on humanity, God offers a promise of hope and redemption through a future Savior. This prophecy introduces several key themes that are central to the Christian understanding of salvation.

1. The Seed of the Woman: The prophecy points to a specific descendant of Eve who will defeat the serpent. This "seed" is identified in the New Testament as Jesus Christ.

2. The Battle Between Good and Evil: The enmity between the serpent and the woman's offspring symbolizes

the spiritual battle that culminates in Christ's victory over sin and Satan.

3. The Ultimate Victory: The crushing of the serpent's head by the woman's offspring signifies the ultimate triumph of Jesus over Satan, sin, and death.

Fulfillment in Jesus Christ

The New Testament identifies Jesus as the fulfillment of the promise made in Genesis 3:15. Several passages highlight this connection and the realization of God's redemptive plan through Christ.

1. Galatians 4:4-5 (NIV): "But when the set time had fully come, God sent his Son, born of a woman, born under the law, to redeem those under the law, that we might receive adoption to sonship."

- Born of a woman: Paul emphasizes Jesus' humanity and His role as the promised seed of the woman.

- To redeem: Jesus' mission is to redeem humanity from the curse of sin, fulfilling the promise of Genesis 3:15.

2. Hebrews 2:14 (NIV): "Since the children have flesh and blood, he too shared in their humanity so that by his death he might break the power of him who holds the power of death—that is, the devil."

- Break the power of the devil: Jesus' death and resurrection defeat Satan, fulfilling the promise of crushing the serpent's head.

3. 1 John 3:8 (NIV): "The reason the Son of God appeared was to destroy the devil's work."

- Destroy the devil's work: Jesus' incarnation and victory over sin and death are the ultimate fulfillment of the Protoevangelium.

Theological Implications

1. God's Redemptive Plan: Genesis 3:15 reveals that God's plan for redemption was established immediately after the fall. It underscores God's sovereignty and His commitment to restoring humanity.

2. The Promise of a Savior: The prophecy points to Jesus as the Savior who would defeat sin and Satan. This early promise sets the stage for the unfolding narrative of salvation throughout the Bible.

3. The Victory of Christ: The crushing of the serpent's head signifies the definitive victory of Jesus over the forces of evil. This victory is central to the Christian faith, offering hope and assurance of salvation.

Conclusion

Genesis 3:15, known as the Protoevangelium, is a foundational prophecy that introduces the promise of a

Savior immediately after the fall of humanity. This verse foreshadows the coming of Jesus Christ, who would ultimately defeat sin and Satan through His death and resurrection. The New Testament affirms Jesus as the fulfillment of this promise, highlighting His role as the Redeemer and Victor over evil. Understanding Genesis 3:15 enriches our appreciation of God's redemptive plan and the centrality of Jesus in the biblical narrative. Through this prophecy, we see the profound hope and assurance that God offers to humanity, even in the midst of judgment.

The Protoevangelium in Early Christian Thought

Early Christian writers and theologians recognized Genesis 3:15 as the first announcement of the gospel. They saw it as a divine promise of redemption that pointed directly to Christ. For example, Irenaeus, an early Church Father, referred to Jesus as the "second Adam" who would undo the damage caused by the first Adam's disobedience. This early recognition of Genesis 3:15 as a messianic prophecy underscores its importance in Christian theology.

Typology and Fulfillment

Throughout the Old Testament, various typological figures and events prefigure the ultimate fulfillment of the Protoevangelium in Jesus. For instance:

1. The Sacrifice of Isaac (Genesis 22): Abraham's willingness to sacrifice his son Isaac foreshadows God's sacrifice of His own Son, Jesus. Just as Isaac is spared by the provision of a ram, humanity is spared through the sacrifice of Jesus.

2. Moses and the Exodus: Moses leads the Israelites out of slavery in Egypt, prefiguring Jesus leading humanity out of the bondage of sin. The Passover lamb in the Exodus narrative is a type of Christ, the Lamb of God who takes away the sin of the world.

Continued Enmity and Ultimate Victory

The enmity between the serpent and the woman's offspring continues throughout biblical history and culminates in the New Testament. Jesus' ministry, death, and resurrection are the ultimate expressions of this conflict and victory.

1. Temptation in the Wilderness (Matthew 4:1-11): Jesus' temptation by Satan in the wilderness mirrors the enmity described in Genesis 3:15. Jesus' triumph over these temptations foreshadows His ultimate victory over sin and Satan.

2. Crucifixion and Resurrection (John 19-20): The crucifixion represents the serpent striking Jesus' heel, causing Him temporary suffering and death. However, the

resurrection signifies Jesus crushing the serpent's head, achieving a decisive and eternal victory.

Application to Believers

The Protoevangelium has profound implications for believers today. It reminds us of God's sovereign plan and His commitment to our redemption. The promise of Genesis 3:15 assures us that:

1. Victory Over Sin: Jesus' victory over sin and Satan is available to all who believe in Him. We are no longer bound by sin but are freed to live in the victory Christ has won.

2. Hope in Suffering: Just as Jesus

' suffering led to victory, our trials can lead to growth and ultimate triumph through Him. We can face challenges with the assurance that God's plan is at work in our lives.

3. Participation in God's Plan: Believers are called to participate in God's redemptive plan by spreading the gospel and living out the victory of Christ in our daily lives.

Conclusion

The Protoevangelium in Genesis 3:15 is a pivotal prophecy that introduces God's redemptive plan immediately after the fall. It points to Jesus Christ as the promised Savior who would defeat sin and Satan. The fulfillment of this prophecy in the New Testament underscores the continuity and coherence of God's salvation plan throughout the

Scriptures. By understanding the Protoevangelium, we gain deeper insights into the nature of God, the mission of Jesus, and the hope and assurance that come from His victory. This foundational promise assures us of God's unwavering commitment to redeem and restore humanity, offering profound hope and encouragement to believers throughout all generations.

How the Promise of Salvation Through Jesus Was Established in Genesis

The book of Genesis, as the first book of the Bible, lays the foundation for the entire biblical narrative. It is within Genesis that we first encounter the promise of salvation, which is ultimately fulfilled in Jesus Christ. This chapter explores how the promise of salvation through Jesus is established in Genesis, examining key events and figures that foreshadow and point to the coming Messiah. Through this exploration, we will see the coherence and continuity of God's redemptive plan from the very beginning.

The Protoevangelium: The First Gospel (Genesis 3:15)

Genesis 3:15 (NIV): "And I will put enmity between you and the woman, and between your offspring and hers; he will crush your head, and you will strike his heel."

Context and Analysis

After the fall of humanity, God pronounces judgments on Adam, Eve, and the serpent. Genesis 3:15, often called the Protoevangelium, or "first gospel," is part of the curse on the serpent. However, it also contains a promise of hope and redemption for humanity.

1. Enmity Between the Serpent and the Woman: This signifies ongoing spiritual conflict between Satan and humanity.

2. Offspring: The offspring of the woman refers both collectively to humanity and specifically to a future individual who will deliver a decisive blow to the serpent.

3. Crushing the Head: The promised individual will ultimately defeat Satan, delivering a fatal blow.

4. Striking the Heel: Satan will inflict harm, but it will not be a decisive or permanent defeat.

This prophecy is fulfilled in Jesus Christ, who defeats Satan through His death and resurrection.

New Testament Fulfillment

- Galatians 4:4-5 (NIV): "But when the set time had fully come, God sent his Son, born of a woman, born under the law, to redeem those under the law, that we might receive adoption to sonship."

- Hebrews 2:14 (NIV): "Since the children have flesh and blood, he too shared in their humanity so that by his death he might break the power of him who holds the power of death—that is, the devil."

- 1 John 3:8 (NIV): "The reason the Son of God appeared was to destroy the devil's work."

The Promise to Abraham

Genesis 12:1-3 (NIV): "The Lord had said to Abram, 'Go from your country, your people and your father's household to the land I will show you. I will make you into a great nation, and I will bless you; I will make your name great, and you will be a blessing. I will bless those who bless you, and whoever curses you I will curse; and all peoples on earth will be blessed through you.'"

Context and Analysis

God's call to Abraham marks a pivotal moment in the unfolding of His redemptive plan. The promises made to Abraham include:

1. A Great Nation: God promises to make Abraham's descendants a great nation.

2. Blessing: Abraham will be blessed and will be a blessing to others.

3. Universal Blessing: All peoples on earth will be blessed through Abraham.

The promise of universal blessing finds its ultimate fulfillment in Jesus Christ, a descendant of Abraham, who brings salvation to all nations.

New Testament Fulfillment

- Galatians 3:8 (NIV): "Scripture foresaw that God would justify the Gentiles by faith, and announced the gospel in advance to Abraham: 'All nations will be blessed through you.'"

- Galatians 3:16 (NIV): "The promises were spoken to Abraham and to his seed. Scripture does not say 'and to seeds,' meaning many people, but 'and to your seed,' meaning one person, who is Christ."

- Matthew 1:1 (NIV): "This is the genealogy of Jesus the Messiah the son of David, the son of Abraham."

The Sacrifice of Isaac

Genesis 22:1-2 (NIV): "Some time later God tested Abraham. He said to him, 'Abraham!' 'Here I am,' he replied. Then God said, 'Take your son, your only son, whom you love—Isaac—and go to the region of Moriah. Sacrifice him there as a burnt offering on a mountain I will show you.'"

Context and Analysis

The story of Abraham's willingness to sacrifice his son Isaac is a powerful foreshadowing of God's ultimate sacrifice of His own Son, Jesus.

1. Test of Faith: Abraham's faith is tested to the extreme.

2. Provision of a Substitute: God provides a ram as a substitute for Isaac, sparing his life.

This event prefigures the sacrificial death of Jesus, the Lamb of God, who takes away the sin of the world.

New Testament Fulfillment

- John 1:29 (NIV): "The next day John saw Jesus coming toward him and said, 'Look, the Lamb of God, who takes away the sin of the world!'"

- Romans 8:32 (NIV): "He who did not spare his own Son, but gave him up for us all—how will he not also, along with him, graciously give us all things?"

- Hebrews 11:17-19 (NIV): "By faith Abraham, when God tested him, offered Isaac as a sacrifice. He who had embraced the promises was about to sacrifice his one and only son, even though God had said to him, 'It is through Isaac that your offspring will be reckoned.' Abraham reasoned that God could even raise the dead, and so in a manner of speaking he did receive Isaac back from death."

Jacob's Ladder

Genesis 28:12-13 (NIV): "He had a dream in which he saw a stairway resting on the earth, with its top reaching to heaven, and the angels of God were ascending and descending on it. There above it stood the Lord, and he said: 'I am the Lord, the God of your father Abraham and the God of Isaac. I will give you and your descendants the land on which you are lying.'"

Context and Analysis

Jacob's dream of a ladder or stairway connecting heaven and earth signifies the connection between God and humanity. This vision points to Jesus as the ultimate bridge between heaven and earth.

1. Divine Revelation: God reveals His promise to Jacob, continuing the covenant made with Abraham and Isaac.

2. Connection to Heaven: The ladder symbolizes the connection between the divine and human realms.

Jesus fulfills this vision by being the mediator who reconciles humanity to God.

New Testament Fulfillment

- John 1:51 (NIV): "He then added, 'Very truly I tell you, you will see heaven open, and the angels of God ascending and descending on the Son of Man.'"

- 1 Timothy 2:5 (NIV): "For there is one God and one mediator between God and mankind, the man Christ Jesus."

- Hebrews 9:15 (NIV): "For this reason Christ is the mediator of a new covenant, that those who are called may receive the promised eternal inheritance—now that he has died as a ransom to set them free from the sins committed under the first covenant."

Joseph as a Type of Christ

Genesis 37-50: The story of Joseph is one of betrayal, suffering, and eventual exaltation, which closely parallels the life of Jesus.

Context and Analysis

1. Betrayal and Suffering: Joseph is betrayed by his brothers and sold into slavery, reflecting Jesus' betrayal by Judas and suffering.

2. Exaltation: Joseph rises to a position of power in Egypt, ultimately saving his family from famine. Similarly, Jesus is exalted through His resurrection and brings salvation to humanity.

New Testament Fulfillment

- Acts 7:9-10 (NIV): "Because the patriarchs were jealous of Joseph, they sold him as a slave into Egypt. But God was with him and rescued him from all his troubles; he gave Joseph wisdom and enabled him to gain the goodwill of Pharaoh king of Egypt. So Pharaoh made him ruler over Egypt and all his palace."

- Philippians 2:9-11 (NIV): "Therefore God exalted him to the highest place and gave him the name that is above every name, that at the name of Jesus every knee should bow, in heaven and on earth and under the earth, and every tongue acknowledge that Jesus Christ is Lord, to the glory of God the Father."

- Romans 8:28 (NIV): "And we know that in all things God works for the good of those who love him, who have been called according to his purpose."

The Promised Blessing to Judah

Genesis 49:10 (NIV): "The scepter will not depart from Judah, nor the ruler's staff from between his feet, until he to whom it belongs shall come and the obedience of the nations shall be his."

Context and Analysis

In Jacob's blessing of his sons, he prophesies that a ruler will come from the tribe of Judah who will command the obedience of the nations. This prophecy points to the coming of the Messiah, who is later revealed to be Jesus.

1. Scepter and Ruler's Staff: Symbols of kingship and authority, indicating that Judah's descendants will produce a line of kings.

2. Obedience of the Nations: This ruler will have

a universal reign, commanding the obedience of all people.

New Testament Fulfillment

- Matthew 1:2-3 (NIV): "Abraham was the father of Isaac, Isaac the father of Jacob, Jacob the father of Judah and his brothers, Judah the father of Perez and Zerah, whose mother was Tamar, Perez the father of Hezron, Hezron the father of Ram."

- Revelation 5:5 (NIV): "Then one of the elders said to me, 'Do not weep! See, the Lion of the tribe of Judah, the Root of David, has triumphed. He is able to open the scroll and its seven seals.'"

- Philippians 2:10-11 (NIV): "That at the name of Jesus every knee should bow, in heaven and on earth and under the earth, and every tongue acknowledge that Jesus Christ is Lord, to the glory of God the Father."

Conclusion

The book of Genesis lays the groundwork for the entire biblical narrative, introducing key themes and figures that point to the promise of salvation through Jesus Christ. From the Protoevangelium in Genesis 3:15 to the promises made to Abraham, Isaac, and Jacob, and the typological figures of Isaac, Joseph, and Judah, we see the unfolding of God's redemptive plan. Each of these elements finds its ultimate fulfillment in Jesus, who is the promised Savior, the mediator between God and humanity, and the one who brings blessing and salvation to all nations. Understanding how the promise of salvation was established in Genesis enriches our comprehension of God's sovereign plan and the continuity of the biblical narrative, leading us to a deeper appreciation of Jesus Christ as the fulfillment of all God's promises.

CHAPTER 05

THE "I AM" STATEMENTS OF JESUS

The "I Am" statements of Jesus in the New Testament are profound declarations of His divinity and identity. These statements, particularly prominent in the Gospel of John, connect Jesus directly to the divine name revealed to Moses in the Old Testament. This chapter explores the significance of these statements, their Hebrew roots, and their theological implications.

The Divine Name: "I Am Who I Am"

Exodus 3:14 (NIV): "God said to Moses, 'I AM WHO I AM. This is what you are to say to the Israelites: 'I AM has sent me to you.'"

Hebrew Meaning and Analysis

The Hebrew phrase אֶהְיֶה אֲשֶׁר אֶהְיֶה (Ehyeh-Asher-Ehyeh) can be translated in various ways, including "I am who

I am," "I will be what I will be," and "I am the Existing One." This self-revealed name of God emphasizes His eternal, self-existent, and unchanging nature.

- אֶהְיֶה (Ehyeh, Strong's H1961): The first person singular form of the verb "to be," indicating existence and presence.

- אֲשֶׁר (Asher, Strong's H834): A relative pronoun that can mean "who," "which," or "that."

- Theological Implications: This name reveals God's self-sufficiency, eternal existence, and unchanging nature. It signifies that God is not dependent on anything or anyone else for His existence.

Jesus and the "I Am" Statements

In the New Testament, Jesus uses the phrase "I Am" (Greek: ἐγώ εἰμι, ego eimi) multiple times, making direct connections to the divine name revealed in Exodus. These statements are particularly significant in the Gospel of John.

1. "I Am the Bread of Life" (John 6:35, 48, 51)

John 6:35 (NIV): "Then Jesus declared, 'I am the bread of life. Whoever comes to me will never go hungry, and whoever believes in me will never be thirsty.'"

- Context: Jesus makes this statement after feeding the 5,000, linking Himself to the provision of manna in the wilderness.

- Meaning: Jesus is the essential sustenance for spiritual life. Just as bread is necessary for physical survival, Jesus is necessary for spiritual sustenance and eternal life.

2. "I Am the Light of the World" (John 8:12)

John 8:12 (NIV): "When Jesus spoke again to the people, he said, 'I am the light of the world. Whoever follows me will never walk in darkness, but will have the light of life.'"

- Context: This statement is made during the Feast of Tabernacles, a festival with significant lighting ceremonies.

- Meaning: Jesus is the source of spiritual illumination and guidance. In a world darkened by sin, He brings the light of truth and life.

3. "I Am the Door of the Sheep" (John 10:7, 9)

John 10:7 (NIV): "Therefore Jesus said again, 'Very truly I tell you, I am the gate for the sheep.'"

- Context: Jesus contrasts Himself with false shepherds who exploit the sheep.

- Meaning: Jesus is the entry point to salvation. Through Him, believers gain access to God's kingdom and protection.

4. "I Am the Good Shepherd" (John 10:11, 14)

John 10:11 (NIV): "I am the good shepherd. The good shepherd lays down his life for the sheep."

- Context: This statement contrasts Jesus with hired hands who abandon the sheep.

- Meaning: Jesus is the caring and sacrificial leader of His followers. He knows His sheep and lays down His life for them.

5. "I Am the Resurrection and the Life" (John 11:25)

John 11:25 (NIV): "Jesus said to her, 'I am the resurrection and the life. The one who believes in me will live, even though they die.'"

- Context: Jesus makes this statement before raising Lazarus from the dead.

- Meaning: Jesus has power over life and death. He offers eternal life to all who believe in Him, conquering death through His resurrection.

6. "I Am the Way, the Truth, and the Life" (John 14:6)

John 14:6 (NIV): "Jesus answered, 'I am the way and the truth and the life. No one comes to the Father except through me.'"

- Context: Jesus speaks these words to His disciples during the Last Supper.

- Meaning: Jesus is the exclusive path to God, embodying truth and the source of all life.

7. "I Am the True Vine" (John 15:1, 5)

John 15:1 (NIV): "I am the true vine, and my Father is the gardener."

- Context: Jesus uses the imagery of a vine and branches to describe the relationship between Himself and His disciples.

- Meaning: Jesus is the source of spiritual vitality. Believers must remain connected to Him to bear fruit.

The Ultimate "I Am" Declaration: John 8:58

John 8:58 (NIV): "Very truly I tell you," Jesus answered, "before Abraham was born, I am!"

- Context: Jesus makes this declaration during a heated discussion with the Pharisees about His identity and authority.

- Meaning: By using the phrase "I Am," Jesus directly associates Himself with the divine name revealed to Moses. This statement asserts His pre-existence and divinity, affirming that He is eternal and uncreated.

Strong's Concordance Insights

- I Am (ἐγώ εἰμι, ego eimi, Strong's G1473 and G1510): This Greek phrase is used by Jesus to declare His identity and divinity, directly linking Himself to the divine name "I Am" in Exodus 3:14.

Theological Implications of the "I Am" Statements

1. Divine Identity: Jesus' "I Am" statements unequivocally affirm His divine nature. He is not just a prophet or teacher but God incarnate.

2. Revelation of God's Character: Each "I Am" statement reveals different facets of God's character – His provision, guidance, protection, truth, and life.

3. Mediator of God's Presence: Jesus as "I Am" bridges the gap between humanity and God. Through Him, we experience God's presence, truth, and life.

4. Source of Eternal Life: Jesus' identity as "I Am" underscores His role as the source of eternal life and salvation. Belief in Him is essential for reconciliation with God and eternal life.

Conclusion

The "I Am" statements of Jesus in the New Testament are profound declarations of His divinity and identity, connecting Him directly to the divine name revealed to Moses in Exodus. These statements reveal different aspects of Jesus' nature and mission, affirming His role as the eternal Son of God who offers salvation and eternal life. By understanding the Hebrew roots of "I Am" and the theological implications of Jesus' declarations, we gain a deeper appreciation of His divine authority and the profound mystery of His incarnation.

Jesus, the great "I Am," invites us to know Him, trust Him, and find life in Him.

The Significance of God's Name "I Am" Revealed to Moses in Exodus 3:14 and Its Connection to Jesus

The revelation of God's name "I Am" to Moses in Exodus 3:14 is one of the most profound moments in the Old Testament. This declaration not only reveals God's eternal and self-existent nature but also lays the groundwork for understanding the identity and mission of Jesus Christ in the New Testament. This chapter explores the significance of God's name "I Am," its meaning in the Hebrew context, and its direct connection to Jesus as revealed in the New Testament.

God's Name "I Am" in Exodus 3:14

Exodus 3:14 (NIV): "God said to Moses, 'I AM WHO I AM. This is what you are to say to the Israelites: 'I AM has sent me to you.'"

Context and Analysis

The revelation of God's name occurs during Moses' encounter with the burning bush. God calls Moses to deliver the Israelites from slavery in Egypt, and Moses asks God for His name to validate his mission.

1. The Burning Bush: The bush that burns without being consumed symbolizes God's holy and eternal presence.

2. Moses' Question: Moses asks God what name he should give to the Israelites to authenticate his mission.

3. God's Response: God reveals His name as "I AM WHO I AM" (Hebrew: אֶהְיֶה אֲשֶׁר אֶהְיֶה, Ehyeh-Asher-Ehyeh).

Hebrew Meaning and Theological Implications

- אֶהְיֶה (Ehyeh, Strong's H1961): The first person singular form of the verb "to be," indicating existence and presence.

- אֲשֶׁר (Asher, Strong's H834): A relative pronoun that can mean "who," "which," or "that."

The phrase אֶהְיֶה אֲשֶׁר אֶהְיֶה can be translated in various ways:

- "I am who I am"
- "I will be what I will be"
- "I am what I am"
- "I will become what I choose to become"
- "I am the Existing One"

This name reveals several key attributes of God:

1. Self-Existence: God is self-existent and independent, not contingent upon anything or anyone else.

2. Eternality: God exists outside of time and space, eternal and unchanging.

3. Sovereignty: God has the power to be whatever He chooses to be, indicating His sovereign control over all creation.

Connection to Jesus in the New Testament

The "I Am" statements of Jesus in the New Testament directly connect Him to the divine name revealed to Moses, affirming His divinity and eternal nature. These statements are particularly prominent in the Gospel of John.

1. "I Am the Bread of Life" (John 6:35, 48, 51)

John 6:35 (NIV): "Then Jesus declared, 'I am the bread of life. Whoever comes to me will never go hungry, and whoever believes in me will never be thirsty.'"

- Significance: Jesus presents Himself as the essential sustenance for spiritual life, just as God provided manna in the wilderness.

2. "I Am the Light of the World" (John 8:12)

John 8:12 (NIV): "When Jesus spoke again to the people, he said, 'I am the light of the world. Whoever follows me will never walk in darkness, but will have the light of life.'"

- Significance: Jesus declares Himself the source of spiritual illumination and guidance, echoing God's presence as the pillar of fire leading Israel through the desert.

3. "I Am the Door of the Sheep" (John 10:7, 9)

John 10:7 (NIV): "Therefore Jesus said again, 'Very truly I tell you, I am the gate for the sheep.'"

- Significance: Jesus is the entry point to salvation, emphasizing His role as the mediator between God and humanity.

4. "I Am the Good Shepherd" (John 10:11, 14)

John 10:11 (NIV): "I am the good shepherd. The good shepherd lays down his life for the sheep."

- Significance: Jesus is the caring and sacrificial leader who knows His followers intimately and gives His life for them, fulfilling the shepherd imagery of the Old Testament.

5. "I Am the Resurrection and the Life" (John 11:25)

John 11:25 (NIV): "Jesus said to her, 'I am the resurrection and the life. The one who believes in me will live, even though they die.'"

- Significance: Jesus asserts His power over life and death, offering eternal life to all who believe in Him.

6. "I Am the Way, the Truth, and the Life" (John 14:6)

John 14:6 (NIV): "Jesus answered, 'I am the way and the truth and the life. No one comes to the Father except through me.'"

- Significance: Jesus declares Himself the exclusive path to God, embodying the ultimate truth and source of life.

7. "I Am the True Vine" (John 15:1, 5)

John 15:1 (NIV): "I am the true vine, and my Father is the gardener."

- Significance: Jesus is the source of spiritual vitality and growth, emphasizing the importance of remaining connected to Him.

The Ultimate "I Am" Declaration: John 8:58

John 8:58 (NIV): "Very truly I tell you," Jesus answered, "before Abraham was born, I am!"

- Context: Jesus makes this declaration during a heated discussion with the Pharisees about His identity and authority.

- Meaning: By using the phrase "I Am," Jesus directly associates Himself with the divine name revealed to Moses. This statement asserts His pre-existence and divinity, affirming that He is eternal and uncreated.

Strong's Concordance Insights

- I Am (ἐγώ εἰμι, ego eimi, Strong's G1473 and G1510): This Greek phrase is used by Jesus to declare His identity and divinity, directly linking Himself to the divine name "I Am" in Exodus 3:14.

Theological Implications

1. Affirmation of Divinity: Jesus' use of "I Am" unequivocally affirms His divine nature, identifying Himself with the God of the Old Testament.

2. Eternal Existence: Jesus' declarations highlight His eternal existence, pre-dating Abraham and existing before the creation of the world.

3. Revelation of God's Character: Each "I Am" statement reveals different facets of God's character – His provision, guidance, protection, truth, and life – all embodied in Jesus.

4. Mediator of God's Presence: Jesus, as "I Am," bridges the gap between humanity and God. Through Him, believers experience God's presence, truth, and life.

5. Source of Eternal Life: Jesus' identity as "I Am" underscores His role as the source of eternal life and salvation. Belief in Him is essential for reconciliation with God and eternal life.

Conclusion

The significance of God's name "I Am" revealed to Moses in Exodus 3:14 is profound, revealing God's self-existence, eternality, and sovereignty. Jesus' use of "I Am" in the New Testament directly connects Him to this divine name, affirming His divinity and eternal nature. These statements provide a deep insight into the identity and mission of Jesus, emphasizing His role as the mediator between God and humanity and the source of eternal life. By understanding the connection between the divine name in the

Old Testament and Jesus' declarations in the New Testament, we gain a richer understanding of the continuity and coherence of God's redemptive plan and the centrality of Jesus in it.

Jesus' Declaration of Divinity Through the Use of "I Am"

The "I Am" statements made by Jesus in the New Testament are powerful declarations of His divinity. By using this phrase, Jesus connects Himself directly to the divine name revealed to Moses in Exodus 3:14. This chapter explores the significance of Jesus' use of "I Am," why it provoked such a strong reaction from the Pharisees, and why they accused Him of making Himself equal to God.

The Significance of "I Am"

Exodus 3:14 (NIV): "God said to Moses, 'I AM WHO I AM. This is what you are to say to the Israelites: 'I AM has sent me to you.'"

Hebrew Meaning and Theological Implications

The Hebrew phrase אֶהְיֶה אֲשֶׁר אֶהְיֶה (Ehyeh-Asher-Ehyeh) can be translated as "I am who I am," "I will be what I will be," or "I am the Existing One." This name signifies God's eternal, self-existent, and unchanging nature.

- Self-Existence: God is self-sufficient, not dependent on anything or anyone.

- Eternality: God exists beyond time, eternal and unchanging.

- Sovereignty: God has absolute authority and power over all creation.

Jesus' Use of "I Am" in the New Testament

Jesus uses the phrase "I Am" (Greek: ἐγώ εἰμι, ego eimi) multiple times in the Gospel of John, making direct connections to the divine name and asserting His divinity.

John 8:58 (NIV): "Very truly I tell you," Jesus answered, "before Abraham was born, I am!"

Context and Analysis

1. Pre-Existence: By stating "before Abraham was born, I am," Jesus asserts His existence before Abraham, indicating His eternal nature.

2. Divine Identity: Using "I Am" directly associates Jesus with the divine name revealed to Moses, making a clear claim to divinity.

3. Eternal Present: The use of "I Am" (present tense) rather than "I was" emphasizes the ongoing and eternal nature of Jesus' existence.

Other "I Am" Statements

1. "I Am the Bread of Life" (John 6:35)

2. "I Am the Light of the World" (John 8:12)

3. "I Am the Door of the Sheep" (John 10:7)

4. "I Am the Good Shepherd" (John 10:11)

5. "I Am the Resurrection and the Life" (John 11:25)

6. "I Am the Way, the Truth, and the Life" (John 14:6)

7. "I Am the True Vine" (John 15:1)

Each of these statements reveals different aspects of Jesus' divine identity and mission, affirming His role as God incarnate.

The Pharisees' Reaction

John 8:59 (NIV): "At this, they picked up stones to stone him, but Jesus hid himself, slipping away from the temple grounds."

Why the Declaration Provoked the Pharisees

1. Blasphemy: According to Jewish law, claiming to be God or equating oneself with God was considered blasphemy, punishable by death (Leviticus 24:16).

2. Authority and Identity: Jesus' declaration challenged the religious authority and identity of the Pharisees, threatening their understanding of God and their own positions of power.

3. Direct Claim to Divinity: By using "I Am," Jesus made an unequivocal claim to divinity, which the Pharisees saw as a direct challenge to the monotheistic belief central to Judaism.

John 10:31-33 (NIV):

31 Again his Jewish opponents picked up stones to stone him,

32 but Jesus said to them, "I have shown you many good works from the Father. For which of these do you stone me?"

33 "We are not stoning you for any good work," they replied, "but for blasphemy, because you, a mere man, claim to be God."

The Pharisees' Accusation

1. Claiming to Be God: The Pharisees understood that Jesus' use of "I Am" was a direct claim to be God. This was not just a matter of semantics but a profound theological declaration.

2. Blasphemy: The Pharisees saw Jesus' claim as blasphemous because it directly contradicted their understanding of God's singular, indivisible nature.

3. Challenge to Authority: Jesus' declarations undermined the Pharisees' religious authority and interpretation of the Scriptures, presenting a radical new understanding of God's nature and presence.

Theological Implications of Jesus' "I Am" Declarations

1. Affirmation of Divinity: Jesus' "I Am" statements unequivocally affirm His divine nature. He is not merely a prophet or teacher but God incarnate.

2. Revelation of God's Character: Each "I Am" statement reveals different facets of God's character – His provision, guidance, protection, truth, and life – all embodied in Jesus.

3. Mediator of God's Presence: Jesus, as "I Am," bridges the gap between humanity and God. Through Him, believers experience God's presence, truth, and life.

4. Source of Eternal Life: Jesus' identity as "I Am" underscores His role as the source of eternal life and salvation. Belief in Him is essential for reconciliation with God and eternal life.

John 14:6 (NIV): "Jesus answered, 'I am the way and the truth and the life. No one comes to the Father except through me.'"

John 11:25 (NIV): "Jesus said to her, 'I am the resurrection and the life. The one who believes in me will live, even though they die.'"

These declarations highlight Jesus as the exclusive path to God and the source of eternal life, emphasizing His divine authority and essential role in salvation.

Conclusion

Jesus' use of "I Am" in the New Testament is a profound declaration of His divinity, directly linking Him to the divine name revealed to Moses in Exodus 3:14. This connection affirms Jesus' eternal, self-existent nature and His unique role as the mediator between God and humanity. The strong reaction from the Pharisees, who accused Jesus of blasphemy and sought to kill Him, underscores the radical and transformative nature of His claims. Understanding the significance of Jesus' "I Am" statements enriches our comprehension of His divine identity and the depth of His mission to bring salvation to the world. Through these declarations, Jesus reveals Himself as the living God, the eternal "I Am," who invites us to know Him, trust Him, and find eternal life in Him.

CHAPTER 06

JESUS AS THE SEED OF ABRAHAM

The promise to Abraham is one of the foundational pillars of the biblical narrative, pointing forward to the coming of the Messiah. Jesus Christ is the ultimate fulfillment of the promises made to Abraham. This chapter explores the significance of Jesus as the seed of Abraham, the promises given to Abraham, how these promises find their fulfillment in Jesus, and the intriguing figure of Melchizedek who foreshadows Christ.

The Promises to Abraham

Genesis 12:1-3 (NIV):

1 The Lord had said to Abram, "Go from your country, your people and your father's household to the land I will show you.

2 I will make you into a great nation, and I will bless you; I will make your name great, and you will be a blessing.

3 I will bless those who bless you, and whoever curses you I will curse; and all peoples on earth will be blessed through you."

Genesis 22:18 (NIV):

"And through your offspring all nations on earth will be blessed, because you have obeyed me."

Context and Analysis

1. A Great Nation: God promises to make Abraham's descendants into a great nation, Israel, through whom He would work His redemptive plan.

2. Blessing and Name: Abraham would be blessed, his name made great, and he would be a blessing to others.

3. Universal Blessing: The promise culminates in the assurance that all peoples on earth will be blessed through Abraham's offspring.

Fulfillment in Jesus Christ

The New Testament explicitly identifies Jesus as the fulfillment of the promises made to Abraham. Jesus, a descendant of Abraham, brings the promised blessing to all nations through His life, death, and resurrection.

Galatians 3:16 (NIV): "The promises were spoken to Abraham and to his seed. Scripture does not say 'and to seeds,' meaning many people, but 'and to your seed,' meaning one person, who is Christ."

1. Jesus as the Seed: Paul clarifies that the promises to Abraham were ultimately fulfilled in Jesus, the singular seed through whom the blessing to all nations would come.

2. Blessing to All Nations: Through Jesus, the blessing promised to Abraham extends to all humanity, offering salvation and reconciliation with God.

Galatians 3:29 (NIV): "If you belong to Christ, then you are Abraham's seed, and heirs according to the promise."

Abraham and the Pre-incarnate Christ

Genesis 18:1-2 (NIV):

1 The Lord appeared to Abraham near the great trees of Mamre while he was sitting at the entrance to his tent in the heat of the day.

2 Abraham looked up and saw three men standing nearby. When he saw them, he hurried from the entrance of his tent to meet them and bowed low to the ground.

Context and Analysis

In Genesis 18, Abraham encounters three visitors, one of whom is identified as the Lord (YHWH). This appearance is considered by many scholars as a theophany, a pre-incarnate appearance of Christ.

1. Theophany: A visible manifestation of God to humanity, often considered an appearance of the pre-incarnate Christ.

2. Divine Promise: During this visit, the Lord reaffirms His promise to Abraham regarding the birth of Isaac, through whom the line to the Messiah would continue.

John 8:56 (NIV): "Your father Abraham rejoiced at the thought of seeing my day; he saw it and was glad."

- Jesus' Declaration: Jesus indicates that Abraham foresaw the coming of the Messiah and rejoiced. This suggests a spiritual insight given to Abraham regarding the future fulfillment of God's promises through Christ.

Melchizedek: A Foreshadowing of Christ

Genesis 14:18-20 (NIV):

18 Then Melchizedek king of Salem brought out bread and wine. He was priest of God Most High,

19 and he blessed Abram, saying, "Blessed be Abram by God Most High, Creator of heaven and earth.

20 And praise be to God Most High, who delivered your enemies into your hand." Then Abram gave him a tenth of everything.

Who Was Melchizedek?

1. King and Priest: Melchizedek is introduced as both king of Salem (peace) and priest of God Most High. This dual role is unique and significant.

2. Type of Christ: Melchizedek is a type, or foreshadowing, of Christ. His priesthood and kingship

prefigure the dual roles of Jesus as our eternal High Priest and King of Kings.

Hebrews 7:1-3 (NIV):

1 This Melchizedek was king of Salem and priest of God Most High. He met Abraham returning from the defeat of the kings and blessed him,

2 and Abraham gave him a tenth of everything. First, the name Melchizedek means "king of righteousness"; then also, "king of Salem" means "king of peace."

3 Without father or mother, without genealogy, without beginning of days or end of life, resembling the Son of God, he remains a priest forever.

Theological Significance

1. King of Righteousness and Peace: Melchizedek's name and title highlight key attributes of Christ. Jesus is the King of Righteousness and the Prince of Peace.

2. Eternal Priesthood: The lack of genealogy for Melchizedek suggests an eternal priesthood, pointing to Jesus' eternal priesthood, which supersedes the Levitical priesthood.

3. Priesthood of Jesus: Hebrews 7 explains that Jesus is a priest in the order of Melchizedek, establishing a new and eternal priesthood based on His perfect and indestructible life.

Hebrews 7:23-25 (NIV):

23 Now there have been many of those priests, since death prevented them from continuing in office;

24 but because Jesus lives forever, he has a permanent priesthood.

25 Therefore he is able to save completely those who come to God through him, because he always lives to intercede for them.

Conclusion

The promise to Abraham finds its ultimate fulfillment in Jesus Christ, the seed through whom all nations are blessed. The encounters Abraham had with God, particularly the theophany in Genesis 18 and the interaction with Melchizedek, provide deep insights into the nature and mission of Jesus. Melchizedek, as a type of Christ, foreshadows the eternal priesthood and kingship of Jesus, highlighting the continuity and fulfillment of God's redemptive plan. By understanding these connections, we gain a richer appreciation of the profound unity and purpose woven throughout the Scriptures, culminating in the person and work of Jesus Christ, the promised Savior and eternal High Priest.

How Jesus is the Ultimate Blessing to All Nations

The promise that all nations would be blessed through Abraham's offspring finds its ultimate fulfillment in Jesus Christ. This chapter explores how Jesus, as the seed of Abraham, brings blessing to all nations, highlighting the biblical teachings and key verses that illustrate this profound truth. Through an expository study and comprehensive commentary, enriched by insights from Strong's Concordance, we will delve into the theological significance of Jesus as the ultimate blessing to all nations.

The Promise to Abraham

Genesis 12:1-3 (NIV):

1 The Lord had said to Abram, "Go from your country, your people and your father's household to the land I will show you.

2 I will make you into a great nation, and I will bless you; I will make your name great, and you will be a blessing.

3 I will bless those who bless you, and whoever curses you I will curse; and all peoples on earth will be blessed through you."

Genesis 22:18 (NIV):

"And through your offspring all nations on earth will be blessed, because you have obeyed me."

Context and Analysis

1. A Great Nation: God promises to make Abraham's descendants into a great nation, Israel, through whom He would work His redemptive plan.

2. Blessing and Name: Abraham would be blessed, his name made great, and he would be a blessing to others.

3. Universal Blessing: The promise culminates in the assurance that all peoples on earth will be blessed through Abraham's offspring.

Strong's Concordance Insights

- Bless (בָּרַךְ, barak, Strong's H1288): To bless, praise, or salute. It signifies favor and endowment of good things.

- Offspring (זֶרַע, zera, Strong's H2233): Seed, descendants, progeny. It can refer to a singular descendant or a collective group.

Jesus as the Fulfillment of the Promise

The New Testament explicitly identifies Jesus as the fulfillment of the promises made to Abraham. Jesus, a descendant of Abraham, brings the promised blessing to all nations through His life, death, and resurrection.

Galatians 3:16 (NIV): "The promises were spoken to Abraham and to his seed. Scripture does not say 'and to seeds,' meaning many people, but 'and to your seed,' meaning one person, who is Christ."

Galatians 3:29 (NIV): "If you belong to Christ, then you are Abraham's seed, and heirs according to the promise."

Expository Study and Commentary

1. Singular Seed: Paul clarifies that the promises to Abraham were ultimately fulfilled in Jesus, the singular seed through whom the blessing to all nations would come.

2. Heirs of the Promise: Believers in Christ are considered Abraham's seed and heirs according to the promise, sharing in the blessings promised to Abraham.

Universal Blessing Through Jesus

1. Salvation and Redemption: Jesus' primary mission was to bring salvation to all humanity. His sacrifice on the cross provided the means for the forgiveness of sins and reconciliation with God.

John 3:16 (NIV): "For God so loved the world that he gave his one and only Son, that whoever believes in him shall not perish but have eternal life."

- Significance: Jesus' sacrifice is the ultimate act of love, offering eternal life to all who believe.

Romans 3:23-24 (NIV): "For all have sinned and fall short of the glory of God, and all are justified freely by his grace through the redemption that came by Christ Jesus."

- Significance: Jesus' redemptive work justifies and restores humanity, fulfilling the promise of blessing to all nations.

2. Inclusion of the Gentiles: Jesus' ministry broke down the barriers between Jews and Gentiles, extending the blessings of God's covenant to all people.

Ephesians 2:13-14 (NIV): "But now in Christ Jesus you who once were far away have been brought near by the blood of Christ. For he himself is our peace, who has made the two groups one and has destroyed the barrier, the dividing wall of hostility."

- Significance: Jesus unites all people, breaking down ethnic and cultural divisions, fulfilling the promise of universal blessing.

Acts 10:34-35 (NIV): "Then Peter began to speak: 'I now realize how true it is that God does not show favoritism but accepts from every nation the one who fears him and does what is right.'"

- Significance: The gospel of Jesus Christ is inclusive, welcoming all who fear God and do what is right.

3. The Great Commission: Jesus' command to His disciples to spread the gospel to all nations underscores His role as the ultimate blessing to all people.

Matthew 28:18-20 (NIV): "Then Jesus came to them and said, 'All authority in heaven and on earth has been given to me. Therefore go and make disciples of all nations, baptizing them in the name of the Father and of the Son and of the Holy Spirit, and teaching them to obey everything I have commanded you. And surely I am with you always, to the very end of the age.'"

- Significance: The Great Commission highlights the global scope of Jesus' mission, ensuring that the blessing promised to Abraham reaches all nations.

4. Transformation and Hope: Jesus brings transformation and hope to individuals and societies, fulfilling the promise of blessing through spiritual renewal and social justice.

2 Corinthians 5:17 (NIV): "Therefore, if anyone is in Christ, the new creation has come: The old has gone, the new is here!"

- Significance: Jesus transforms lives, making believers new creations who reflect God's love and justice in the world.

Luke 4:18-19 (NIV): "The Spirit of the Lord is on me, because he has anointed me to proclaim good news to the poor. He has sent me to proclaim freedom for the prisoners and recovery of sight for the blind, to set the oppressed free, to proclaim the year of the Lord's favor."

- Significance: Jesus' ministry brings comprehensive blessing, addressing spiritual, physical, and social needs.

Theological Implications

1. Jesus as the Fulfillment of God's Promises: Jesus' life, death, and resurrection fulfill the promises made to Abraham, demonstrating God's faithfulness and sovereign plan.

2. Inclusivity of the Gospel: The gospel of Jesus Christ is for all nations, breaking down barriers and extending God's blessings to all people.

3. Transformation and Hope: Jesus brings transformation and hope to individuals and societies, reflecting the comprehensive nature of God's blessing.

4. Eternal Impact: The blessings through Jesus are not temporal but eternal, offering everlasting life and reconciliation with God.

Conclusion

Jesus Christ is the ultimate fulfillment of the promises made to Abraham, bringing blessing to all nations. Through His life, death, and resurrection, Jesus provides salvation, includes the Gentiles in God's covenant, and commissions His followers to spread the gospel to all people. The theological implications of Jesus as the seed of Abraham underscore God's faithfulness and the inclusivity of the gospel. Jesus, the ultimate blessing, transforms lives and societies, offering eternal hope and reconciliation with God. Understanding how Jesus fulfills the promises to Abraham enriches our appreciation of God's redemptive plan and the profound unity of the biblical narrative.

Paul's Explanation in Galatians 3:16 – The Promise to Abraham's Seed, Which is Christ

In his letter to the Galatians, Paul provides a profound theological exposition on the promise made to Abraham and its ultimate fulfillment in Jesus Christ. Galatians 3:16 is a key verse where Paul explains that the promise was made to Abraham's "seed," which is Christ. This chapter delves into Paul's explanation, the significance of his argument, and why he used this teaching to address the church in Galatia.

Paul's Explanation in Galatians 3:16

Galatians 3:16 (NIV): "The promises were spoken to Abraham and to his seed. Scripture does not say 'and to seeds,' meaning many people, but 'and to your seed,' meaning one person, who is Christ."

Context and Analysis

Paul's argument in Galatians centers on the nature of God's promise to Abraham and its fulfillment. He emphasizes the singular form of "seed" to highlight that the promises were ultimately fulfilled in one person—Christ.

1. Singular Seed: Paul points out that the promise was made to Abraham's "seed" (Greek: σπέρμα, sperma, Strong's G4690), not "seeds," indicating a single descendant rather than many.

2. Christ as the Seed: Paul identifies Christ as the singular seed to whom the promises were made. This interpretation underscores that Jesus is the ultimate fulfillment of God's promise to Abraham.

Strong's Concordance Insights

- Seed (σπέρμα, sperma, Strong's G4690): Refers to offspring, descendant, or progeny. Paul uses the singular form to emphasize the unique role of Christ in fulfilling the promise.

- Promise (ἐπαγγελία, epangelia, Strong's G1860): Refers to a divine assurance of good. The promises to Abraham are seen as guarantees of God's blessings, fulfilled in Christ.

Theological Significance of Paul's Argument

1. Fulfillment of the Promise: Paul's explanation emphasizes that the ultimate fulfillment of God's promise to Abraham is found in Jesus Christ. This fulfillment is not

through the many descendants of Abraham (Israel) but through one particular descendant—Christ.

2. Christ-Centered Interpretation: Paul's argument reinterprets the Abrahamic covenant in a Christ-centered way, showing that Jesus is the focal point of God's redemptive plan.

3. Unity of Scripture: Paul's interpretation highlights the unity and continuity of Scripture, connecting the Old Testament promises with their New Testament fulfillment in Christ.

Why Paul Used This Teaching in Galatia

Context of the Letter to the Galatians

The Galatian church was dealing with significant theological and practical issues, primarily revolving around the influence of Judaizers—those who taught that Gentile Christians must observe the Mosaic Law to be truly saved. Paul's letter addresses these issues directly.

1. Judaizers' Influence: The Judaizers were insisting that Gentile believers in Galatia must adhere to Jewish laws and customs, particularly circumcision, to be part of God's covenant people.

2. Paul's Defense of Justification by Faith: Paul wrote to defend the doctrine of justification by faith alone, apart from the works of the Law.

Galatians 3:6-9 (NIV):

6 So also Abraham "believed God, and it was credited to him as righteousness."

7 Understand, then, that those who have faith are children of Abraham.

8 Scripture foresaw that God would justify the Gentiles by faith, and announced the gospel in advance to Abraham: "All nations will be blessed through you."

9 So those who rely on faith are blessed along with Abraham, the man of faith.

Paul's Argument

1. Faith and Righteousness: Paul emphasizes that Abraham's righteousness came through faith, not through the Law. This establishes a precedent for justification by faith.

2. Inclusion of the Gentiles: By identifying Christ as the seed of Abraham, Paul underscores that the blessings of the Abrahamic covenant are available to all who have faith in Christ, including Gentiles.

3. Opposition to Legalism: Paul's argument aims to counter the legalistic teachings of the Judaizers, affirming that adherence to the Mosaic Law is not required for salvation.

Galatians 3:26-29 (NIV):

26 So in Christ Jesus you are all children of God through faith,

27 for all of you who were baptized into Christ have clothed yourselves with Christ.

28 There is neither Jew nor Gentile, neither slave nor free, nor is there male and female, for you are all one in Christ Jesus.

29 If you belong to Christ, then you are Abraham's seed, and heirs according to the promise.

Significance for the Galatian Church

1. Unity in Christ: Paul's teaching emphasizes the unity of all believers in Christ, breaking down ethnic, social, and gender barriers. All who belong to Christ are Abraham's seed and heirs of the promise.

2. Freedom from the Law: By focusing on faith in Christ as the basis for being heirs of the promise, Paul liberates the Galatians from the obligation to observe the Mosaic Law.

3. Assurance of Salvation: Paul assures the Galatian believers that their salvation and inclusion in God's covenant people are secure through faith in Christ alone.

Expository Study and Comprehensive Commentary Galatians 3:6-14 (NIV):

6 So also Abraham "believed God, and it was credited to him as righteousness."

7 Understand, then, that those who have faith are children of Abraham.

8 Scripture foresaw that God would justify the Gentiles by faith, and announced the gospel in advance to Abraham: "All nations will be blessed through you."

9 So those who rely on faith are blessed along with Abraham, the man of faith.

10 For all who rely on the works of the law are under a curse, as it is written: "Cursed is everyone who does not continue to do everything written in the Book of the Law."

11 Clearly no one who relies on the law is justified before God, because "the righteous will live by faith."

12 The law is not based on faith; on the contrary, it says, "The person who does these things will live by them."

13 Christ redeemed us from the curse of the law by becoming a curse for us, for it is written: "Cursed is everyone who is hung on a pole."

14 He redeemed us in order that the blessing given to Abraham might come to the Gentiles through Christ Jesus, so that by faith we might receive the promise of the Spirit.

Key Points

1. Justification by Faith: Paul emphasizes that justification comes through faith, just as Abraham was justified by believing God.

2. Inclusion of the Gentiles: The blessing of Abraham extends to the Gentiles through faith in Christ, fulfilling the promise that all nations would be blessed through Abraham's seed.

3. Christ's Redemption: Jesus redeemed humanity from the curse of the Law by becoming a curse for us, enabling the blessing of Abraham to come to all who believe.

Strong's Concordance Insights

- Faith (πίστις, pistis, Strong's G4102): Firm persuasion, conviction, or belief in the truth, particularly reliance upon Christ for salvation.

- Righteousness (δικαιοσύνη, dikaiosyne, Strong's G1343): The state of being just or right, often understood as the condition acceptable to God.

Conclusion

Paul's explanation in Galatians 3:16 that the promise was made to Abraham's "seed," which is Christ, is a profound theological declaration that emphasizes the fulfillment of God's covenant through Jesus. Paul uses this teaching to address the church in Galatia, countering the influence of Judaizers and affirming the doctrine of justification by faith. By identifying Christ as the singular seed of Abraham, Paul underscores the inclusivity of the gospel, the unity of all believers in Christ, and the freedom from the Mosaic Law.

This teaching not only solidifies the connection between the Old and New Testaments but also provides assurance and hope to believers that they are heirs of God's promises through faith in Jesus Christ.

CHAPTER 07

THE SACFRIFICE OF ISAAC AND JESUS

The story of Abraham's willingness to sacrifice his son Isaac is one of the most profound and dramatic narratives in the Old Testament. Found in Genesis 22, this event is not only a test of Abraham's faith but also a powerful foreshadowing of the ultimate sacrifice of Jesus Christ. This chapter explores the parallels between the near-sacrifice of Isaac and the crucifixion of Jesus, highlighting how this Old Testament event prefigures the New Testament fulfillment.

The Story of Abraham and Isaac

Genesis 22:1-2 (NIV):

1 Some time later God tested Abraham. He said to him, "Abraham!" "Here I am," he replied.

2 Then God said, "Take your son, your only son, whom you love—Isaac—and go to the region of Moriah.

Sacrifice him there as a burnt offering on a mountain I will show you."

Context and Analysis

1. God's Test: The chapter begins with God testing Abraham's faith and obedience by asking him to sacrifice his beloved son, Isaac.

2. The Command: God's instruction is explicit and challenging: Abraham must take Isaac to Mount Moriah and offer him as a burnt offering.

Genesis 22:3-5 (NIV):

3 Early the next morning Abraham got up and loaded his donkey. He took with him two of his servants and his son Isaac. When he had cut enough wood for the burnt offering, he set out for the place God had told him about.

4 On the third day Abraham looked up and saw the place in the distance.

5 He said to his servants, "Stay here with the donkey while I and the boy go over there. We will worship and then we will come back to you."

Faith and Obedience

1. Immediate Obedience: Abraham's immediate response to God's command demonstrates his unwavering faith and obedience.

2. Prophetic Statement: Abraham's statement to his servants, "We will worship and then we will come back to you," suggests his faith that God would somehow preserve Isaac.

Genesis 22:6-8 (NIV):

6 Abraham took the wood for the burnt offering and placed it on his son Isaac, and he himself carried the fire and the knife. As the two of them went on together,

7 Isaac spoke up and said to his father Abraham, "Father?" "Yes, my son?" Abraham replied. "The fire and wood are here," Isaac said, "but where is the lamb for the burnt offering?"

8 Abraham answered, "God himself will provide the lamb for the burnt offering, my son." And the two of them went on together.

Symbolism and Foreshadowing

1. Isaac Carrying the Wood: Isaac carrying the wood for his own sacrifice parallels Jesus carrying the cross.

2. God's Provision: Abraham's statement, "God himself will provide the lamb," foreshadows the ultimate provision of Jesus as the Lamb of God.

Genesis 22:9-12 (NIV):

9 When they reached the place God had told him about, Abraham built an altar there and arranged the wood on

it. He bound his son Isaac and laid him on the altar, on top of the wood.

10 Then he reached out his hand and took the knife to slay his son.

11 But the angel of the Lord called out to him from heaven, "Abraham! Abraham!" "Here I am," he replied.

12 "Do not lay a hand on the boy," he said. "Do not do anything to him. Now I know that you fear God, because you have not withheld from me your son, your only son."

Divine Intervention

1. Test of Faith: Abraham's willingness to sacrifice Isaac demonstrates his absolute trust in God.

2. God's Intervention: God intervenes at the last moment, sparing Isaac and affirming Abraham's faith.

Genesis 22:13-14 (NIV):

13 Abraham looked up and there in a thicket he saw a ram caught by its horns. He went over and took the ram and sacrificed it as a burnt offering instead of his son.

14 So Abraham called that place The Lord Will Provide. And to this day it is said, "On the mountain of the Lord it will be provided."

God's Provision

1. Substitute Sacrifice: The ram provided by God as a substitute for Isaac prefigures Jesus, who is the ultimate substitute for humanity.

2. The Lord Will Provide: The name Abraham gives to the place highlights God's provision and foreshadows the ultimate provision of Jesus.

Parallels Between Isaac and Jesus

Only Son

1. Isaac: Referred to as Abraham's "only son" (Genesis 22:2, 12, 16), highlighting his unique and beloved status.

2. Jesus: Described as God's "one and only Son" (John 3:16), underscoring His unique and divine nature.

Willing Sacrifice

1. Isaac: Isaac's willingness to carry the wood and be bound on the altar mirrors Jesus' willing submission to the Father's will.

2. Jesus: Jesus willingly laid down His life, submitting to the Father's plan for salvation (John 10:17-18).

Carrying the Wood

1. Isaac: Carries the wood for his own sacrifice up Mount Moriah.

2. Jesus: Carries His cross to Golgotha (John 19:17).

Divine Provision

1. Isaac: A ram is provided as a substitute for Isaac.

2. Jesus: Jesus is the Lamb of God, provided as a substitute for humanity (John 1:29).

Resurrection Imagery

1. Isaac: Abraham's faith that God could raise Isaac from the dead (Hebrews 11:19) parallels the resurrection of Jesus.

2. Jesus: Jesus' actual resurrection from the dead, confirming His victory over sin and death (1 Corinthians 15:3-4).

Theological Significance

1. Test of Faith and Obedience: The story of Abraham and Isaac highlights the importance of faith and obedience to God's commands, even when they are difficult to understand.

2. Foreshadowing of Christ's Sacrifice: The parallels between Isaac's near-sacrifice and Jesus' crucifixion illustrate the consistency and continuity of God's redemptive plan.

3. Divine Provision and Substitution: The provision of the ram as a substitute for Isaac foreshadows the substitutionary atonement of Jesus, who takes upon Himself the sins of the world.

Hebrews 11:17-19 (NIV):

17 By faith Abraham, when God tested him, offered Isaac as a sacrifice. He who had embraced the promises was about to sacrifice his one and only son,

18 even though God had said to him, "It is through Isaac that your offspring will be reckoned."

19 Abraham reasoned that God could even raise the dead, and so in a manner of speaking he did receive Isaac back from death.

Strong's Concordance Insights

- Faith (πίστις, pistis, Strong's G4102): Firm persuasion, conviction, or belief in the truth, particularly reliance upon Christ for salvation.

- Provide (רָאָה, ra'ah, Strong's H7200): To see, perceive, or provide. In the context of Genesis 22:14, it signifies God's provision.

Conclusion

The story of Abraham's willingness to sacrifice Isaac is a powerful foreshadowing of Jesus' ultimate sacrifice. The parallels between Isaac and Jesus highlight the consistency and continuity of God's redemptive plan. Through the near-sacrifice of Isaac, we see a glimpse of the ultimate provision God would make in Jesus Christ, the Lamb of God who takes away the sin of the world. This profound narrative underscores the themes of faith, obedience, divine provision, and substitutionary atonement, enriching our understanding of God's plan for salvation and the central role of Jesus in fulfilling that plan. By examining these parallels, we gain a deeper appreciation of the interconnectedness of Scripture and the depth of God's love and sacrifice for humanity.

Parallels Between Isaac's Near-Sacrifice and Jesus' Crucifixion

The story of Abraham's willingness to sacrifice Isaac in Genesis 22 is rich with symbolism that foreshadows the ultimate sacrifice of Jesus Christ. This chapter explores the numerous parallels between Isaac's near-sacrifice and Jesus' crucifixion, highlighting how this Old Testament narrative prefigures the New Testament fulfillment of God's redemptive plan through Jesus.

The Command to Sacrifice

Genesis 22:1-2 (NIV):

1 Some time later God tested Abraham. He said to him, "Abraham!" "Here I am," he replied.

2 Then God said, "Take your son, your only son, whom you love—Isaac—and go to the region of Moriah. Sacrifice him there as a burnt offering on a mountain I will show you."

Parallel with Jesus

- Only Son:

- Isaac: Referred to as Abraham's "only son" (Genesis 22:2, 12, 16), highlighting his unique and beloved status.

- Jesus: Described as God's "one and only Son" (John 3:16), underscoring His unique and divine nature.

John 3:16 (NIV): "For God so loved the world that he gave his one and only Son, that whoever believes in him shall not perish but have eternal life."

The Journey to the Sacrifice

Genesis 22:3-4 (NIV):

3 Early the next morning Abraham got up and loaded his donkey. He took with him two of his servants and his son Isaac. When he had cut enough wood for the burnt offering, he set out for the place God had told him about.

4 On the third day Abraham looked up and saw the place in the distance.

Parallel with Jesus

- Three-Day Journey:

- Isaac: The journey to Mount Moriah took three days (Genesis 22:4), symbolically representing a period of death and resurrection.

- Jesus: Jesus was in the tomb for three days before His resurrection (Matthew 12:40).

Matthew 12:40 (NIV): "For as Jonah was three days and three nights in the belly of a huge fish, so the Son of Man will be three days and three nights in the heart of the earth."

Carrying the Wood

Genesis 22:6 (NIV):

6 Abraham took the wood for the burnt offering and placed it on his son Isaac, and he himself carried the fire and the knife. As the two of them went on together,

Parallel with Jesus

- Carrying the Wood:

 - Isaac: Isaac carried the wood for his own sacrifice (Genesis 22:6).

 - Jesus: Jesus carried His cross to Golgotha (John 19:17).

John 19:17 (NIV): "Carrying his own cross, he went out to the place of the Skull (which in Aramaic is called Golgotha)."

The Willingness to Sacrifice

Genesis 22:9-10 (NIV):

9 When they reached the place God had told him about, Abraham built an altar there and arranged the wood on it. He bound his son Isaac and laid him on the altar, on top of the wood.

10 Then he reached out his hand and took the knife to slay his son.

Parallel with Jesus

- Willing Submission:

- Isaac: Isaac's willingness to be bound and laid on the altar mirrors Jesus' willing submission to the Father's will (Genesis 22:9-10).

- Jesus: Jesus willingly laid down His life, submitting to the Father's plan for salvation (John 10:17-18).

John 10:17-18 (NIV): "The reason my Father loves me is that I lay down my life—only to take it up again. No one takes it from me, but I lay it down of my own accord. I have authority to lay it down and authority to take it up again. This command I received from my Father."

The Substitutionary Sacrifice

Genesis 22:11-13 (NIV):

11 But the angel of the Lord called out to him from heaven, "Abraham! Abraham!" "Here I am," he replied.

12 "Do not lay a hand on the boy," he said. "Do not do anything to him. Now I know that you fear God, because you have not withheld from me your son, your only son."

13 Abraham looked up and there in a thicket he saw a ram caught by its horns. He went over and took the ram and sacrificed it as a burnt offering instead of his son.

Parallel with Jesus

- Substitute Sacrifice:

- Isaac: A ram was provided as a substitute for Isaac, sparing his life (Genesis 22:13).

- Jesus: Jesus is the Lamb of God, provided as a substitute for humanity, taking upon Himself the sins of the world (John 1:29).

John 1:29 (NIV): "The next day John saw Jesus coming toward him and said, 'Look, the Lamb of God, who takes away the sin of the world!'"

The Place of Sacrifice

Genesis 22:2 (NIV): "Then God said, 'Take your son, your only son, whom you love—Isaac—and go to the region of Moriah. Sacrifice him there as a burnt offering on a mountain I will show you.'"

Parallel with Jesus

- Mount Moriah and Golgotha:

- Isaac: The region of Moriah, where Isaac was to be sacrificed, is traditionally believed to be the area where Jerusalem was later built, and specifically the site of the Temple Mount.

- Jesus: Jesus was crucified at Golgotha, located just outside the walls of Jerusalem, fulfilling the typology of the sacrificial lamb.

The Faith of Abraham and the Resurrection

Genesis 22:5 (NIV): "He said to his servants, 'Stay here with the donkey while I and the boy go over there. We will worship and then we will come back to you.'"

Parallel with Jesus

- Faith in Resurrection:

- Isaac: Abraham's statement, "We will come back to you," indicates his faith that God could raise Isaac from the dead if necessary (Hebrews 11:19).

- Jesus: Jesus' resurrection from the dead confirmed His victory over sin and death (1 Corinthians 15:3-4).

Hebrews 11:19 (NIV): "Abraham reasoned that God could even raise the dead, and so in a manner of speaking he did receive Isaac back from death."

1 Corinthians 15:3-4 (NIV): "For what I received I passed on to you as of first importance: that Christ died for our sins according to the Scriptures, that he was buried, that he was raised on the third day according to the Scriptures."

The Promise of Blessing

Genesis 22:15-18 (NIV):

15 The angel of the Lord called to Abraham from heaven a second time

16 and said, "I swear by myself, declares the Lord, that because you have done this and have not withheld your son, your only son,

17 I will surely bless you and make your descendants as numerous as the stars in the sky and as the sand on the seashore. Your descendants will take possession of the cities of their enemies,

18 and through your offspring all nations on earth will be blessed, because you have obeyed me."

Parallel with Jesus

- Universal Blessing:

- Isaac: The promise that all nations would be blessed through Abraham's offspring is reaffirmed after Isaac is spared (Genesis 22:18).

- Jesus: Jesus, as the seed of Abraham, fulfills this promise by bringing salvation to all nations (Galatians 3:16).

Galatians 3:16 (NIV): "The promises were spoken to Abraham and to his seed. Scripture does not say 'and to seeds,' meaning many people, but 'and to your seed,' meaning one person, who is Christ."

Theological Implications

1. Typology of Sacrifice: The near-sacrifice of Isaac serves as a typology of Christ's sacrifice, highlighting themes of substitution, obedience, and divine provision.

2. Foreshadowing Christ's Atonement: The narrative foreshadows the ultimate atonement provided by Jesus, the Lamb of God, who takes away the sins of the world.

3. Faith and Obedience: Abraham's faith and obedience are paralleled in Jesus' willing submission to the Father's will, demonstrating the ultimate act of faith and obedience.

Romans 4:3 (NIV): "What does Scripture say? 'Abraham believed God, and it was credited to him as righteousness.'"

Philippians 2:8 (NIV): "And being found in appearance as a man, he humbled himself by becoming obedient to death—even death on a cross!"

Conclusion

The story of Abraham's willingness to sacrifice Isaac is rich with parallels to the crucifixion of Jesus Christ. These parallels highlight the consistency and continuity of God's redemptive plan. Through the near-sacrifice of Isaac, we see a powerful foreshadowing of the ultimate sacrifice made by Jesus, the Lamb of God. By examining these parallels, we gain a deeper understanding of the interconnectedness of Scripture and the profound significance of Jesus' atoning work on the cross. This narrative underscores themes of faith, obedience, divine provision, and substitutionary atonement, enriching our appreciation of God's love and sacrifice for humanity.

CHAPTER 08

THE CONCEPT OF SUBSTITUTIONARY ATONEMENT

Substitutionary atonement is a foundational doctrine in Christian theology that explains how Jesus' death on the cross pays the penalty for sin on behalf of humanity. This chapter explores the concept of substitutionary atonement, its biblical basis, and why it is imperative for understanding the significance of Jesus' death. We will delve into key scriptural passages, provide comprehensive commentary, and examine how this doctrine reveals the depth of God's love and justice.

What is Substitutionary Atonement?

Substitutionary atonement is the theological concept that Jesus Christ, by His death on the cross, took the place of sinners, bearing the punishment that was rightfully theirs.

This act satisfies the demands of God's justice while demonstrating His profound love and mercy.

1. Substitution: Jesus stands in the place of sinners, enduring the penalty of sin on their behalf.

2. Atonement: Jesus' sacrificial death reconciles humanity to God, removing the barrier of sin.

Key Aspects:

- Penal Substitution: Jesus takes the punishment for sin that humanity deserves.

- Sacrificial Lamb: Jesus is the ultimate sacrifice, fulfilling the Old Testament sacrificial system.

- Redemption and Reconciliation: Jesus' death redeems humanity from sin and reconciles them to God.

Biblical Basis for Substitutionary Atonement

Isaiah 53:4-6 (NIV):

4 Surely he took up our pain and bore our suffering,
    yet we considered him punished by God,
    stricken by him, and afflicted.
5 But he was pierced for our transgressions,
    he was crushed for our iniquities;
    the punishment that brought us peace was on him,
    and by his wounds we are healed.
6 We all, like sheep, have gone astray,
    each of us has turned to our own way;

and the Lord has laid on him

the iniquity of us all.

Expository Study and Commentary:

1. Vicarious Suffering: The Suffering Servant takes upon Himself the pain and suffering of others.

2. Pierced for Our Transgressions: The Servant's suffering is a direct result of humanity's sins.

3. Substitutionary Act: The Lord lays the iniquity of humanity on the Servant, signifying substitution.

Strong's Concordance Insights:

- Transgressions (פֶּשַׁע, pesha, Strong's H6588): Rebellion or sin.

- Iniquities (עָוֹן, avon, Strong's H5771): Guilt or moral evil.

1 Peter 2:24 (NIV): "He himself bore our sins in his body on the cross, so that we might die to sins and live for righteousness; by his wounds you have been healed."

Expository Study and Commentary:

1. Bearing Sins: Jesus takes the sins of humanity upon Himself, bearing them in His body on the cross.

2. Purpose: Jesus' sacrificial act enables believers to die to sin and live for righteousness.

3. Healing through Suffering: The wounds of Jesus bring spiritual healing and restoration.

Romans 3:23-25 (NIV):

23 For all have sinned and fall short of the glory of God,

24 and all are justified freely by his grace through the redemption that came by Christ Jesus.

25 God presented Christ as a sacrifice of atonement, through the shedding of his blood—to be received by faith. He did this to demonstrate his righteousness, because in his forbearance he had left the sins committed beforehand unpunished—

Expository Study and Commentary:

1. Universal Sinfulness: All humanity is guilty of sin and falls short of God's glory.

2. Justification by Grace: Believers are justified freely by God's grace through the redemption in Christ.

3. Atoning Sacrifice: Jesus is presented as a sacrifice of atonement, demonstrating God's righteousness and justice.

Strong's Concordance Insights:

- Atonement (ἱλαστήριον, hilasterion, Strong's G2435): Propitiation or expiatory sacrifice, signifying an offering that appeases God's wrath and brings reconciliation.

2 Corinthians 5:21 (NIV): "God made him who had no sin to be sin for us, so that in him we might become the righteousness of God."

Expository Study and Commentary:

1. Sinless Substitute: Jesus, who knew no sin, was made to be sin for humanity.

2. Imputed Righteousness: Believers receive the righteousness of God through Jesus' sacrificial act.

3. Divine Exchange: This verse highlights the divine exchange—Jesus takes on humanity's sin, and believers receive His righteousness.

The Imperative Nature of Substitutionary Atonement in Jesus' Death

1. Satisfaction of Divine Justice: God's justice demands that sin be punished. Jesus' substitutionary death satisfies this requirement, upholding the holiness and justice of God.

Romans 6:23 (NIV): "For the wages of sin is death, but the gift of God is eternal life in Christ Jesus our Lord."

- Wages of Sin: Sin earns death, the ultimate penalty.

- Gift of God: Through Jesus, the penalty is paid, and believers receive eternal life.

2. Expression of Divine Love: Substitutionary atonement is the ultimate expression of God's love. By taking humanity's place, Jesus demonstrates God's immense love for His creation.

John 15:13 (NIV): "Greater love has no one than this: to lay down one's life for one's friends."

- Ultimate Sacrifice: Jesus' willingness to lay down His life exemplifies the greatest act of love.

3. Reconciliation with God: Jesus' death bridges the gap between sinful humanity and a holy God, making reconciliation possible.

Colossians 1:21-22 (NIV):

21 Once you were alienated from God and were enemies in your minds because of your evil behavior.

22 But now he has reconciled you by Christ's physical body through death to present you holy in his sight, without blemish and free from accusation—

- Reconciliation through Death: Jesus' physical death reconciles believers to God, making them holy and blameless.

4. Redemption from Sin: Jesus' substitutionary death redeems believers from the bondage of sin, setting them free.

Ephesians 1:7 (NIV): "In him we have redemption through his blood, the forgiveness of sins, in accordance with the riches of God's grace."

- Redemption and Forgiveness: Through Jesus' blood, believers are redeemed and their sins forgiven.

Theological Implications

1. God's Justice and Mercy: Substitutionary atonement upholds God's justice by ensuring that sin is punished, while simultaneously demonstrating His mercy by providing a substitute.

2. Imputed Righteousness: Believers are credited with the righteousness of Christ, transforming their standing before God.

3. Transformation and Sanctification: The believer's life is transformed through Jesus' atoning work, leading to sanctification and a new way of living.

Romans 5:8-9 (NIV):

8 But God demonstrates his own love for us in this: While we were still sinners, Christ died for us.

9 Since we have now been justified by his blood, how much more shall we be saved from God's wrath through him!

- Demonstration of Love: Jesus' death while humanity was still in sin showcases God's proactive love.

- Justification and Salvation: Justification by Jesus' blood saves believers from God's wrath.

Conclusion

The concept of substitutionary atonement is central to understanding the significance of Jesus' death. Through His sacrificial act, Jesus takes the place of sinners, bearing the punishment for sin and satisfying the demands of divine justice. This profound doctrine underscores the depth of God's love, the necessity of Christ's atoning work, and the transformation it brings to believers. By examining key biblical passages and their theological implications, we gain a deeper appreciation of the immense sacrifice made by Jesus and the incredible gift of salvation offered to humanity. Jesus' death on the cross is the ultimate act of substitutionary atonement, reconciling humanity to God and securing eternal life for all who believe.

Jacob's Ladder and Jesus

Jacob's dream of a ladder reaching to heaven, as recorded in Genesis 28:12, is a significant and symbolic event in the biblical narrative. This chapter explores the importance of Jacob's dream, the symbolism of the ladder, and how this Old Testament vision points to the person and work of Jesus Christ in the New Testament. By examining the dream and its fulfillment in Jesus, we gain a deeper understanding of God's redemptive plan and the connection between heaven and earth.

Jacob's Dream: The Biblical Account

Genesis 28:10-12 (NIV):

10 Jacob left Beersheba and set out for Harran.

11 When he reached a certain place, he stopped for the night because the sun had set. Taking one of the stones there, he put it under his head and lay down to sleep.

12 He had a dream in which he saw a stairway resting on the earth, with its top reaching to heaven, and the angels of God were ascending and descending on it.

Context and Analysis

1. Jacob's Journey: Jacob is traveling from Beersheba to Harran to escape his brother Esau's anger and to find a wife among his relatives.

2. The Dream: In his dream, Jacob sees a ladder or stairway that reaches from earth to heaven, with angels ascending and descending on it.

3. Divine Encounter: The dream represents a divine encounter where God reaffirms His covenant promises to Jacob, which were originally made to Abraham and Isaac.

Genesis 28:13-15 (NIV):

13 There above it stood the Lord, and he said: "I am the Lord, the God of your father Abraham and the God of Isaac. I will give you and your descendants the land on which you are lying.

14 Your descendants will be like the dust of the earth, and you will spread out to the west and to the east, to the

north and to the south. All peoples on earth will be blessed through you and your offspring.

15 I am with you and will watch over you wherever you go, and I will bring you back to this land. I will not leave you until I have done what I have promised you."

The Significance of Jacob's Dream

1. Affirmation of the Covenant: God reaffirms the covenant promises made to Abraham and Isaac, assuring Jacob of his role in God's plan.

2. God's Presence and Protection: The dream emphasizes God's ongoing presence and protection over Jacob, despite his circumstances.

3. Connection Between Heaven and Earth: The ladder symbolizes the connection between heaven and earth, indicating that God is actively involved in the affairs of humanity.

Genesis 28:16-17 (NIV):

16 When Jacob awoke from his sleep, he thought, "Surely the Lord is in this place, and I was not aware of it."

17 He was afraid and said, "How awesome is this place! This is none other than the house of God; this is the gate of heaven."

Jacob's Response:

1.   Recognition of God's Presence: Jacob acknowledges the presence of God in that place, calling it the house of God and the gate of heaven.

2. Reverence and Awe: Jacob's fear and awe reflect the significance of encountering God and recognizing the sacredness of the place.

The Ladder as a Symbol

1. Connection Between Heaven and Earth: The ladder represents the connection between the divine and the human realms, showing that God is not distant but intimately involved in the world.

2. Access to God: The ladder signifies access to God, with angels serving as messengers between heaven and earth, indicating that God communicates with and cares for His people.

3. Foreshadowing of Christ: The ladder serves as a typological foreshadowing of Jesus Christ, who is the ultimate bridge between heaven and earth.

Fulfillment in Jesus Christ

John 1:51 (NIV): "He then added, 'Very truly I tell you, you will see heaven open, and the angels of God ascending and descending on the Son of Man.'"

Expository Study and Commentary:

1. Jesus as the Ladder: In John 1:51, Jesus refers to Himself as the fulfillment of Jacob's ladder. He is the bridge that connects heaven and earth, providing access to God.

2. Angels Ascending and Descending: The imagery of angels ascending and descending on Jesus signifies His role as the mediator between God and humanity.

Strong's Concordance Insights:

- Ascending (ἀναβαίνω, anabaino, Strong's G305): To go up, ascend.

- Descending (καταβαίνω, katabaino, Strong's G2597): To come down, descend.

- Son of Man (ὁ υἱὸς τοῦ ἀνθρώπου, ho huios tou anthrōpou, Strong's G5207 and G444): A title Jesus used for Himself, emphasizing His humanity and messianic role.

Theological Implications of the Ladder and Jesus

1. Mediator Between God and Humanity: Jesus is the ultimate mediator, bridging the gap between a holy God and sinful humanity. His life, death, and resurrection provide the way for humanity to be reconciled with God.

1 Timothy 2:5 (NIV): "For there is one God and one mediator between God and mankind, the man Christ Jesus."

2. Access to God's Presence: Through Jesus, believers have direct access to God's presence, without the need for intermediaries.

Ephesians 2:18 (NIV): "For through him we both have access to the Father by one Spirit."

3. Fulfillment of God's Promises: Jesus fulfills the promises made to Abraham, Isaac, and Jacob, bringing the blessings of the covenant to all nations.

Galatians 3:14 (NIV): "He redeemed us in order that the blessing given to Abraham might come to the Gentiles through Christ Jesus, so that by faith we might receive the promise of the Spirit."

4. God's Active Involvement: The imagery of angels ascending and descending emphasizes God's ongoing involvement in the world and His active communication with humanity through Jesus.

Hebrews 1:1-2 (NIV):

1 In the past God spoke to our ancestors through the prophets at many times and in various ways,

2 but in these last days he has spoken to us by his Son, whom he appointed heir of all things, and through whom also he made the universe.

Conclusion

Jacob's dream of a ladder reaching to heaven is a profound and significant vision that reveals the connection between heaven and earth. This ladder symbolizes access to God and foreshadows the coming of Jesus Christ, who is the ultimate bridge between the divine and human realms. Jesus' declaration in John 1:51 confirms that He is the fulfillment of this vision, serving as the mediator who reconciles humanity to God. Through Jesus, believers have direct access to God's presence, fulfilling the covenant promises and demonstrating God's active involvement in the world. Understanding the significance of Jacob's ladder and its fulfillment in Jesus enriches our appreciation of God's redemptive plan and the central role of Christ in connecting heaven and earth.

Jesus as the Bridge Between Heaven and Earth

The concept of Jesus as the bridge between heaven and earth is beautifully encapsulated in John 1:51. This imagery not only highlights Jesus' unique role as the mediator between God and humanity but also reflects the fulfillment of various Old Testament symbols and prophecies. This chapter explores the significance of Jesus as the bridge, focusing on John 1:51, and delves into how this understanding enriches our comprehension of His divine mission.

Jesus' Declaration in John 1:51

John 1:51 (NIV): "He then added, 'Very truly I tell you, you will see heaven open, and the angels of God ascending and descending on the Son of Man.'"

Context and Analysis

1. Context: Jesus speaks these words to Nathanael, one of His early disciples, who is amazed by Jesus' supernatural knowledge about him.

2. Angels Ascending and Descending: This imagery recalls Jacob's dream in Genesis 28:12, where he saw a ladder reaching to heaven with angels ascending and descending on it.

3. Son of Man: Jesus uses the title "Son of Man," which emphasizes His role as the Messiah and His connection to humanity.

Strong's Concordance Insights:

- Ascending (ἀναβαίνω, anabaino, Strong's G305): To go up, ascend.

- Descending (καταβαίνω, katabaino, Strong's G2597): To come down, descend.

- Son of Man (ὁ υἱὸς τοῦ ἀνθρώπου, ho huios tou anthrōpou, Strong's G5207 and G444): A title Jesus used for Himself, emphasizing His humanity and messianic role.

The Significance of Jesus as the Bridge

1. Mediator Between God and Humanity:

1 Timothy 2:5 (NIV): "For there is one God and one mediator between God and mankind, the man Christ Jesus."

- Explanation: Jesus is the sole mediator who bridges the gap between a holy God and sinful humanity. His life, death, and resurrection enable direct access to God.

2. Fulfillment of Jacob's Ladder:

Genesis 28:12 (NIV): "He had a dream in which he saw a stairway resting on the earth, with its top reaching to heaven, and the angels of God were ascending and descending on it."

- Explanation: Jacob's ladder symbolizes the connection between heaven and earth. Jesus fulfills this vision, becoming the ultimate means of connection between God and humanity.

3. Access to God's Presence:

Ephesians 2:18 (NIV): "For through him we both have access to the Father by one Spirit."

- Explanation: Jesus provides believers with direct access to the Father, breaking down the barriers that separated humanity from God.

4. The Revelation of God's Glory:

John 1:14 (NIV): "The Word became flesh and made his dwelling among us. We have seen his glory, the glory of the one and only Son, who came from the Father, full of grace and truth."

- Explanation: Jesus, as the Word made flesh, reveals God's glory and brings divine grace and truth to humanity.

Theological Implications

1. Incarnation and Revelation:

- Incarnation: Jesus, as God incarnate, embodies the divine presence on earth. He is the tangible manifestation of God's glory and love.

- Revelation: Through Jesus, God reveals His character, will, and redemptive plan.

2. Redemption and Reconciliation:

- Redemption: Jesus' sacrificial death redeems humanity from sin, fulfilling the requirements of divine justice.

- Reconciliation: Through Jesus, humanity is reconciled to God, restoring the broken relationship caused by sin.

2 Corinthians 5:18-19 (NIV):

18 All this is from God, who reconciled us to himself through Christ and gave us the ministry of reconciliation:

19 that God was reconciling the world to himself in Christ, not counting people's sins against them. And he has committed to us the message of reconciliation.

- Explanation: Jesus' work of reconciliation brings peace between God and humanity, allowing believers to become ambassadors of this reconciliation.

3. New Covenant:

- Explanation: Jesus establishes a new covenant through His blood, providing a direct and permanent relationship with God.

Luke 22:20 (NIV): "In the same way, after the supper he took the cup, saying, 'This cup is the new covenant in my blood, which is poured out for you.'"

- Explanation: The new covenant is characterized by grace and truth, fulfilled in Jesus' sacrificial act.

Jesus as the Fulfillment of Old Testament Types

1. The Tabernacle and Temple:

- Explanation: Jesus fulfills the function of the Tabernacle and Temple as the dwelling place of God's presence among His people.

John 2:19-21 (NIV):

19 Jesus answered them, "Destroy this temple, and I will raise it again in three days."

20 They replied, "It has taken forty-six years to build this temple, and you are going to raise it in three days?"

21 But the temple he had spoken of was his body.

- Explanation: Jesus' body is the true temple where God's presence dwells, and His resurrection signifies the new, eternal temple.

2. The Sacrificial System:

- Explanation: Jesus is the ultimate sacrifice, fulfilling the Old Testament sacrificial system and providing a once-for-all atonement for sin.

Hebrews 10:10 (NIV): "And by that will, we have been made holy through the sacrifice of the body of Jesus Christ once for all."

- Explanation: Jesus' sacrifice is sufficient to cleanse from sin and bring believers into a holy relationship with God.

3. The High Priest:

- Explanation: Jesus serves as the eternal High Priest, mediating between God and humanity.

Hebrews 4:14-16 (NIV):

14 Therefore, since we have a great high priest who has ascended into heaven, Jesus the Son of God, let us hold firmly to the faith we profess.

15 For we do not have a high priest who is unable to feel sympathy for our weaknesses, but we have one who has been tempted in every way, just as we are—yet he did not sin.

16 Let us then approach God's throne of grace with confidence, so that we may receive mercy and find grace to help us in our time of need.

- Explanation: Jesus' priestly role assures believers of access to God's grace and mercy.

Practical Implications for Believers

1. Assurance of Salvation:

- Explanation: Believers can have confidence in their salvation, knowing that Jesus has secured their relationship with God.

John 10:28-29 (NIV):

28 I give them eternal life, and they shall never perish; no one will snatch them out of my hand.

29 My Father, who has given them to me, is greater than all; no one can snatch them out of my Father's hand.

- Explanation: Jesus' role as the bridge guarantees eternal security for believers.

2. Empowered Prayer Life:

- Explanation: Believers have direct access to God through Jesus, empowering their prayer life.

Hebrews 4:16 (NIV): "Let us then approach God's throne of grace with confidence, so that we may receive mercy and find grace to help us in our time of need."

- Explanation: The confidence to approach God in prayer is grounded in Jesus' mediating work.

3. Mission and Evangelism:

- Explanation: Believers are called to share the message of reconciliation with others, extending the invitation to experience God's grace.

2 Corinthians 5:20 (NIV): "We are therefore Christ's ambassadors, as though God were making his appeal through us. We implore you on Christ's behalf: Be reconciled to God."

- Explanation: As ambassadors of Christ, believers participate in God's mission to reconcile the world to Himself.

Conclusion

Jesus as the bridge between heaven and earth is a profound theological truth that reveals His unique role in God's redemptive plan. Through His life, death, and resurrection, Jesus provides the way for humanity to be reconciled to God, fulfilling the symbolism of Jacob's ladder and numerous Old Testament types. This understanding enriches our comprehension of Jesus' divine mission and its practical implications for believers, offering assurance of salvation, empowering prayer, and motivating mission. By recognizing Jesus as the ultimate mediator, we gain a deeper appreciation of His sacrifice and the access to God's presence that He provides.

The Connection Between the Vision of Jacob and the Mission of Jesus

Jacob's dream of a ladder reaching to heaven in Genesis 28:12 is a pivotal moment in the Old Testament, symbolizing the connection between heaven and earth. This vision finds its ultimate fulfillment in the mission of Jesus Christ, who bridges the gap between God and humanity. This chapter explores the profound connection between Jacob's vision and the mission of Jesus, highlighting key biblical verses and providing comprehensive commentary with insights from Strong's Concordance.

Jacob's Vision: The Biblical Account

Genesis 28:10-12 (NIV):

10 Jacob left Beersheba and set out for Harran.

11 When he reached a certain place, he stopped for the night because the sun had set. Taking one of the stones there, he put it under his head and lay down to sleep.

12 He had a dream in which he saw a stairway resting on the earth, with its top reaching to heaven, and the angels of God were ascending and descending on it.

Context and Analysis

1. Jacob's Journey: Jacob is traveling from Beersheba to Harran to escape his brother Esau's anger and to find a wife among his relatives.

2. The Dream: In his dream, Jacob sees a ladder or stairway that reaches from earth to heaven, with angels ascending and descending on it.

3. Divine Encounter: The dream represents a divine encounter where God reaffirms His covenant promises to Jacob, which were originally made to Abraham and Isaac.

Genesis 28:13-15 (NIV):

13 There above it stood the Lord, and he said: "I am the Lord, the God of your father Abraham and the God of Isaac. I will give you and your descendants the land on which you are lying.

14 Your descendants will be like the dust of the earth, and you will spread out to the west and to the east, to the north and to the south. All peoples on earth will be blessed through you and your offspring.

15 I am with you and will watch over you wherever you go, and I will bring you back to this land. I will not leave you until I have done what I have promised you."

Jacob's Response:

Genesis 28:16-17 (NIV):

16 When Jacob awoke from his sleep, he thought, "Surely the Lord is in this place, and I was not aware of it."

17 He was afraid and said, "How awesome is this place! This is none other than the house of God; this is the gate of heaven."

1. Recognition of God's Presence: Jacob acknowledges the presence of God in that place, calling it the house of God and the gate of heaven.

2. Reverence and Awe: Jacob's fear and awe reflect the significance of encountering God and recognizing the sacredness of the place.

Jesus' Declaration in John 1:51

John 1:51 (NIV): "He then added, 'Very truly I tell you, you will see heaven open, and the angels of God ascending and descending on the Son of Man.'"

Context and Analysis

1. Context: Jesus speaks these words to Nathanael, one of His early disciples, who is amazed by Jesus' supernatural knowledge about him.

2. Angels Ascending and Descending: This imagery recalls Jacob's dream in Genesis 28:12, where he saw a ladder reaching to heaven with angels ascending and descending on it.

3. Son of Man: Jesus uses the title "Son of Man," which emphasizes His role as the Messiah and His connection to humanity.

Strong's Concordance Insights:

- Ascending (ἀναβαίνω, anabaino, Strong's G305): To go up, ascend.

- Descending (καταβαίνω, katabaino, Strong's G2597): To come down, descend.

- Son of Man (ὁ υἱὸς τοῦ ἀνθρώπου, ho huios tou anthrōpou, Strong's G5207 and G444): A title Jesus used for Himself, emphasizing His humanity and messianic role.

The Significance of Jacob's Vision

1. Affirmation of the Covenant: God reaffirms the covenant promises made to Abraham and Isaac, assuring Jacob of his role in God's plan.

2. God's Presence and Protection: The dream emphasizes God's ongoing presence and protection over Jacob, despite his circumstances.

3. Connection Between Heaven and Earth: The ladder symbolizes the connection between heaven and earth, indicating that God is actively involved in the affairs of humanity.

The Fulfillment in Jesus Christ

Jesus as the Ladder:

John 1:51 (NIV): "He then added, 'Very truly I tell you, you will see heaven open, and the angels of God ascending and descending on the Son of Man.'"

1. Jesus as the Bridge: Jesus declares that He is the fulfillment of Jacob's vision, serving as the bridge between heaven and earth.

2. Angels on Jesus: The imagery of angels ascending and descending on the Son of Man signifies that Jesus is the mediator between God and humanity.

Mediator Between God and Humanity:

1 Timothy 2:5 (NIV): "For there is one God and one mediator between God and mankind, the man Christ Jesus."

1. Unique Mediator: Jesus is the sole mediator who bridges the gap between a holy God and sinful humanity.

2. Access to God: Through Jesus, believers have direct access to God's presence.

Reconciliation and Redemption:

Colossians 1:19-20 (NIV):

19 For God was pleased to have all his fullness dwell in him,

20 and through him to reconcile to himself all things, whether things on earth or things in heaven, by making peace through his blood, shed on the cross.

1. Fullness of God: Jesus embodies the fullness of God, making Him the perfect mediator.

2. Peace Through His Blood: Jesus' sacrificial death on the cross brings reconciliation and peace between God and humanity.

Theological Implications

1. Incarnation and Revelation:

   - Incarnation: Jesus, as God incarnate, embodies the divine presence on earth.

   - Revelation: Through Jesus, God reveals His character, will, and redemptive plan.

John 1:14 (NIV): "The Word became flesh and made his dwelling among us. We have seen his glory, the glory of the one and only Son, who came from the Father, full of grace and truth."

2. Redemption and Reconciliation:

   - Redemption: Jesus' sacrificial death redeems humanity from sin.

   - Reconciliation: Through Jesus, humanity is reconciled to God.

2 Corinthians 5:18-19 (NIV):

18 All this is from God, who reconciled us to himself through Christ and gave us the ministry of reconciliation:

19 that God was reconciling the world to himself in Christ, not counting people's sins against them. And he has committed to us the message of reconciliation.

3. New Covenant:

- New Covenant: Jesus establishes a new covenant through His blood.

Luke 22:20 (NIV): "In the same way, after the supper he took the cup, saying, 'This cup is the new covenant in my blood, which is poured out for you.'"

Practical Implications for Believers

1. Assurance of Salvation:

- Assurance: Believers can have confidence in their salvation through Jesus.

John 10:28-29 (NIV):

28 I give them eternal life, and they shall never perish; no one will snatch them out of my hand.

29 My Father, who has given them to me, is greater than all; no one can snatch them out of my Father's hand.

2. Empowered Prayer Life:

- Prayer Life: Believers have direct access to God through Jesus.

Hebrews 4:16 (NIV): "Let us then approach God's throne of grace with confidence, so that we may receive mercy and find grace to help us in our time of need."

3. Mission and Evangelism:

- Mission: Believers are called to share the message of reconciliation.

2 Corinthians 5:20 (NIV): "We are therefore Christ's ambassadors, as though God were making his appeal through us. We implore you on Christ's behalf: Be reconciled to God."

Conclusion

Jacob's vision of a ladder reaching to heaven is a profound symbol of the connection between heaven and earth. This vision finds its ultimate fulfillment in Jesus Christ, who serves as the bridge between God and humanity. Through Jesus, believers have direct access to God's presence, experience reconciliation and redemption, and are assured of their salvation. Understanding the connection between Jacob's vision and the mission of Jesus enriches our appreciation of God's redemptive plan and the central role of Christ in mediating the divine-human relationship. Jesus, the ladder to heaven, reveals God's glory and love, providing a way for all to be reconciled to Him.

CHAPTER 09

JOSEPH AS A TYPE OF CHRIST

The story of Joseph, found in the book of Genesis, is one of the most compelling narratives in the Bible. It is rich with themes of suffering, redemption, and divine providence. Joseph's life prefigures the life and mission of Jesus Christ in numerous ways. This chapter explores the parallels between Joseph and Jesus, comparing their assignments and examining how Joseph serves as a type of Christ. By analyzing key Bible references and providing comprehensive commentary with insights from Strong's Concordance, we can appreciate the profound connection between these two figures.

The Story of Joseph

Genesis 37:3-4 (NIV):

3 Now Israel loved Joseph more than any of his other sons, because he had been born to him in his old age; and he made an ornate robe for him.

4 When his brothers saw that their father loved him more than any of them, they hated him and could not speak a kind word to him.

Context and Analysis

1. Beloved Son: Joseph is dearly loved by his father, Jacob (Israel), and is given a special robe, symbolizing his favored status.

2. Hatred and Envy: Joseph's brothers hate him due to their father's favoritism and Joseph's prophetic dreams, which indicate his future superiority over them.

Genesis 37:23-24 (NIV):

23 So when Joseph came to his brothers, they stripped him of his robe—the ornate robe he was wearing—

24 and they took him and threw him into the cistern. The cistern was empty; there was no water in it.

Betrayal and Suffering

1. Stripped of His Robe: Joseph's brothers strip him of his robe, symbolizing the loss of his favored status.

2. Thrown into the Cistern: Joseph is cast into a pit, a foreshadowing of his descent into suffering and abandonment.

Genesis 37:28 (NIV):

28 So when the Midianite merchants came by, his brothers pulled Joseph up out of the cistern and sold him for twenty shekels of silver to the Ishmaelites, who took him to Egypt.

Sold for Silver

1. Betrayed for Silver: Joseph is sold by his brothers for twenty shekels of silver, indicating betrayal and rejection by his own family.

Strong's Concordance Insights:

- Silver (כֶּסֶף, keseph, Strong's H3701): Money, used in transactions and often symbolizes betrayal or valuation.

Genesis 39:2-4 (NIV):

2 The Lord was with Joseph so that he prospered, and he lived in the house of his Egyptian master.

3 When his master saw that the Lord was with him and that the Lord gave him success in everything he did,

4 Joseph found favor in his eyes and became his attendant. Potiphar put him in charge of his household, and he entrusted to his care everything he owned.

Joseph's Rise and Fall

1. Divine Favor: Despite his circumstances, Joseph finds favor in Egypt due to God's presence with him.

2. Potiphar's House: Joseph rises to a position of responsibility in Potiphar's household, but this success is short-lived due to false accusations.

Genesis 39:20-21 (NIV):

20 Joseph's master took him and put him in prison, the place where the king's prisoners were confined.

21 But while Joseph was there in the prison, the Lord was with him; he showed him kindness and granted him favor in the eyes of the prison warden.

Imprisonment and Hope

1. False Accusations: Joseph is falsely accused by Potiphar's wife and thrown into prison.

2. God's Favor in Prison: Even in prison, God's presence with Joseph leads to favor and responsibilities.

Genesis 41:39-41 (NIV):

39 Then Pharaoh said to Joseph, "Since God has made all this known to you, there is no one so discerning and wise as you.

40 You shall be in charge of my palace, and all my people are to submit to your orders. Only with respect to the throne will I be greater than you."

41 So Pharaoh said to Joseph, "I hereby put you in charge of the whole land of Egypt."

Exaltation and Provision

1. Interpreter of Dreams: Joseph interprets Pharaoh's dreams, foretelling seven years of plenty followed by seven years of famine.

2. Ruler of Egypt: Pharaoh exalts Joseph to a position of authority, second only to himself, making Joseph the savior of Egypt and the surrounding nations during the famine.

Parallels Between Joseph and Jesus

Beloved Son

- Joseph: Beloved son of Jacob, given a special robe (Genesis 37:3).

- Jesus: Beloved Son of God, affirmed by the Father at His baptism (Matthew 3:17).

Matthew 3:17 (NIV): "And a voice from heaven said, 'This is my Son, whom I love; with him I am well pleased.'"

Hated and Rejected by Brothers

- Joseph: Hated by his brothers and sold into slavery (Genesis 37:4, 28).

- Jesus: Rejected by His own people, betrayed by Judas for thirty pieces of silver (John 1:11, Matthew 26:14-15).

John 1:11 (NIV): "He came to that which was his own, but his own did not receive him."

Matthew 26:14-15 (NIV):

14 Then one of the Twelve—the one called Judas Iscariot—went to the chief priests

15 and asked, "What are you willing to give me if I deliver him over to you?" So they counted out for him thirty pieces of silver.

Falsely Accused and Suffered

- Joseph: Falsely accused by Potiphar's wife and imprisoned (Genesis 39:20).

- Jesus: Falsely accused by religious leaders and sentenced to death (Mark 14:55-56).

Mark 14:55-56 (NIV):

55 The chief priests and the whole Sanhedrin were looking for evidence against Jesus so that they could put him to death, but they did not find any.

56 Many testified falsely against him, but their statements did not agree.

Divine Favor and Exaltation

- Joseph: Exalted to a position of power in Egypt, saving many from famine (Genesis 41:39-41).

- Jesus: Exalted to the right hand of God, providing salvation for humanity (Philippians 2:9-11).

Philippians 2:9-11 (NIV):

9 Therefore God exalted him to the highest place and gave him the name that is above every name,

10 that at the name of Jesus every knee should bow, in heaven and on earth and under the earth,

11 and every tongue acknowledge that Jesus Christ is Lord, to the glory of God the Father.

Forgiveness and Reconciliation

- Joseph: Forgives his brothers and reconciles with them, saving them from famine (Genesis 45:4-5).

- Jesus: Offers forgiveness and reconciliation to all who believe, saving them from eternal death (Luke 23:34, Colossians 1:19-20).

Genesis 45:4-5 (NIV):

4 Then Joseph said to his brothers, "Come close to me." When they had done so, he said, "I am your brother Joseph, the one you sold into Egypt!

5 And now, do not be distressed and do not be angry with yourselves for selling me here, because it was to save lives that God sent me ahead of you."

Luke 23:34 (NIV): "Jesus said, 'Father, forgive them, for they do not know what they are doing.' And they divided up his clothes by casting lots."

Colossians 1:19-20 (NIV):

19 For God was pleased to have all his fullness dwell in him,

20 and through him to reconcile to himself all things, whether things on earth or things in heaven, by making peace through his blood, shed on the cross.

Theological Implications

1. God's Sovereignty and Providence: Both stories emphasize God's control over circumstances and His ability to bring about His redemptive purposes through suffering and betrayal.

Romans 8:28 (NIV): "And we know that in all things God works for the good of those who love him, who have been called according to his purpose."

2. Prefiguring Christ's Work: Joseph's life serves as a foreshadowing of Jesus' mission to save humanity, demonstrating themes of suffering, exaltation, and reconciliation.

3. Forgiveness and Redemption: The narrative of Joseph highlights the importance of forgiveness and redemption, pointing to the ultimate forgiveness and redemption offered through Jesus.

Practical Implications for Believers

1. Trust in God's Plan: Believers can trust in God's sovereign plan, even in difficult circumstances, knowing that He can bring good out of evil.

2. Embrace Forgiveness: Just as Joseph forgave his brothers, believers are called to forgive others, following the example of Jesus.

Ephesians 4:32 (NIV): "Be kind and compassionate to one another, forgiving each other, just as in Christ God forgave you."

3. Proclaim Reconciliation: Believers are called to share the message of reconciliation, inviting others to experience the forgiveness and salvation available in Christ.

2 Corinthians 5:18-20 (NIV

18 All this is from God, who reconciled us to himself through Christ and gave us the ministry of reconciliation:

19 that God was reconciling the world to himself in Christ, not counting people's sins against them. And he has committed to us the message of reconciliation.

20 We are therefore Christ's ambassadors, as though God were making his appeal through us. We implore you on Christ's behalf: Be reconciled to God.

Conclusion

The story of Joseph serves as a powerful type of Christ, illustrating key aspects of Jesus' mission and character. Through the parallels between Joseph and Jesus, we see God's sovereign hand at work in history, bringing about redemption and reconciliation. Joseph's life prefigures the suffering, betrayal, exaltation, and ultimate forgiveness offered by Jesus, providing a rich tapestry of themes that point to the greater reality fulfilled in Christ. By understanding these connections, believers can deepen their appreciation of God's redemptive plan and be encouraged to trust in His providence, embrace forgiveness, and proclaim the message of reconciliation to the world.

Joseph's Suffering, Exaltation, and Role as Savior of His People

The narrative of Joseph, found in the latter chapters of Genesis, is a profound and multifaceted story of suffering, redemption, and divine providence. Joseph's journey from favored son to suffering servant, and ultimately to exalted savior of his people, mirrors the life and mission of Jesus Christ. This chapter explores Joseph's suffering, his subsequent exaltation, and his role as the savior of his people, drawing parallels to the life of Jesus and providing comprehensive commentary with insights from Strong's Concordance.

Joseph's Suffering

Genesis 37:3-4 (NIV):

3 Now Israel loved Joseph more than any of his other sons, because he had been born to him in his old age; and he made an ornate robe for him.

4 When his brothers saw that their father loved him more than any of them, they hated him and could not speak a kind word to him.

Beloved Son and Envy

1. Favored by His Father: Joseph is deeply loved by his father Jacob, who gives him a special robe as a sign of his favor.

2. Hatred from Brothers: Joseph's brothers are envious and hateful towards him, unable to speak kindly to him due to their jealousy.

Genesis 37:23-24, 28 (NIV):

23 So when Joseph came to his brothers, they stripped him of his robe—the ornate robe he was wearing—

24 and they took him and threw him into the cistern. The cistern was empty; there was no water in it.

28 So when the Midianite merchants came by, his brothers pulled Joseph up out of the cistern and sold him for twenty shekels of silver to the Ishmaelites, who took him to Egypt.

Betrayal and Sold into Slavery

1. Stripped of His Robe: Joseph's brothers strip him of his robe, symbolizing the loss of his favored status.

2. Thrown into the Cistern: He is cast into a pit, experiencing abandonment and suffering.

3. Sold for Silver: Joseph is sold for twenty shekels of silver, betrayed by his own family.

Strong's Concordance Insights:

- Cistern (בּוֹר, bor, Strong's H953): A pit or well, often used as a prison or place of confinement.

- Silver (כֶּסֶף, keseph, Strong's H3701): Money, often associated with betrayal and valuation.

Genesis 39:2-4, 20 (NIV):

2 The Lord was with Joseph so that he prospered, and he lived in the house of his Egyptian master.

3 When his master saw that the Lord was with him and that the Lord gave him success in everything he did,

4 Joseph found favor in his eyes and became his attendant. Potiphar put him in charge of his household, and he entrusted to his care everything he owned.

20 Joseph's master took him and put him in prison, the place where the king's prisoners were confined.

Falsely Accused and Imprisoned

1. Divine Favor: Despite his circumstances, God's presence with Joseph allows him to prosper in Potiphar's house.

2. False Accusation: Joseph is falsely accused by Potiphar's wife and unjustly imprisoned.

Joseph's Exaltation

Genesis 41:14, 39-41 (NIV):

14 So Pharaoh sent for Joseph, and he was quickly brought from the dungeon. When he had shaved and changed his clothes, he came before Pharaoh.

39 Then Pharaoh said to Joseph, "Since God has made all this known to you, there is no one so discerning and wise as you.

40 You shall be in charge of my palace, and all my people are to submit to your orders. Only with respect to the throne will I be greater than you."

41 So Pharaoh said to Joseph, "I hereby put you in charge of the whole land of Egypt."

Rise to Power

1. Interpreting Pharaoh's Dreams: Joseph's ability to interpret Pharaoh's dreams demonstrates his God-given wisdom.

2. Exalted by Pharaoh: Pharaoh exalts Joseph to a position of great authority, second only to himself, making him the ruler of Egypt.

Strong's Concordance Insights:

- Dream (חֲלוֹם, chalom, Strong's H2472): A vision or revelation often seen as a divine message.

- Exalted (רָמָה, rama, Strong's H7311): To be lifted up or raised in rank.

Genesis 41:46-49 (NIV):

46 Joseph was thirty years old when he entered the service of Pharaoh king of Egypt. And Joseph went out from Pharaoh's presence and traveled throughout Egypt.

47 During the seven years of abundance the land produced plentifully.

48 Joseph collected all the food produced in those seven years of abundance in Egypt and stored it in the cities. In each city he put the food grown in the fields surrounding it.

49 Joseph stored up huge quantities of grain, like the sand of the sea; it was so much that he stopped keeping records because it was beyond measure.

Wisdom and Provision

1. Age and Service: Joseph begins his service at the age of thirty, a significant age in biblical terms often associated with the beginning of public ministry (Jesus also began His ministry at thirty).

2. Preparation for Famine: Joseph wisely prepares for the impending famine by storing surplus grain during the years of abundance.

Joseph's Role as Savior

Genesis 41:56-57 (NIV):

56 When the famine had spread over the whole country, Joseph opened all the storehouses and sold grain to the Egyptians, for the famine was severe throughout Egypt.

57 And all the world came to Egypt to buy grain from Joseph, because the famine was severe everywhere.

Savior of Many

1. Provision During Famine: Joseph's foresight and administrative skills save Egypt and the surrounding nations from starvation.

2. Global Impact: People from all over the world come to Egypt to buy grain, highlighting Joseph's role as a savior beyond just his own people.

Genesis 45:4-8 (NIV):

4 Then Joseph said to his brothers, "Come close to me." When they had done so, he said, "I am your brother Joseph, the one you sold into Egypt!

5 And now, do not be distressed and do not be angry with yourselves for selling me here, because it was to save lives that God sent me ahead of you.

6 For two years now there has been famine in the land, and for the next five years there will be no plowing and reaping.

7 But God sent me ahead of you to preserve for you a remnant on earth and to save your lives by a great deliverance.

8 So then, it was not you who sent me here, but God. He made me father to Pharaoh, lord of his entire household and ruler of all Egypt.

Forgiveness and Reconciliation

1. Revelation to His Brothers: Joseph reveals his identity to his brothers, demonstrating forgiveness and grace.

2. Divine Purpose: Joseph recognizes that God orchestrated his suffering for a greater purpose—to save lives and preserve a remnant.

Parallels to Jesus Christ

Beloved Son and Envy

- Joseph: Beloved by his father, envied and hated by his brothers (Genesis 37:3-4).

- Jesus: Beloved Son of God, rejected by His own people (John 3:16, John 1:11).

Betrayal and Sold

- Joseph: Betrayed and sold by his brothers for silver (Genesis 37:28).

- Jesus: Betrayed by Judas for thirty pieces of silver (Matthew 26:14-15).

Falsely Accused and Suffered

- Joseph: Falsely accused and imprisoned (Genesis 39:20).

- Jesus: Falsely accused and crucified (Mark 14:55-56).

Exalted to Rule

- Joseph: Exalted to rule over Egypt, saving many from famine (Genesis 41:39-41).

- Jesus: Exalted to the right hand of God, providing salvation for humanity (Philippians 2:9-11).

Savior and Reconciliation

- Joseph: Saves his family and many others, reconciles with his brothers (Genesis 45:4-8).

- Jesus: Saves humanity from sin, offers forgiveness and reconciliation (Colossians 1:19-20).

Colossians 1:19-20 (NIV):

19 For God was pleased to have all his fullness dwell in him,

20 and through him to reconcile to himself all things, whether things on earth or things in heaven, by making peace through his blood, shed on the cross.

Theological Implications

1. Sovereignty of God: Both Joseph's and Jesus' stories highlight God's sovereignty in using suffering and evil intentions for a greater redemptive purpose.

Romans 8:28 (NIV): "And we know that in all things God works for the good of those who love him, who have been called according to his purpose."

2. Redemption Through Suffering: The suffering of both Joseph and Jesus leads to the salvation of many, emphasizing the redemptive power of suffering.

3. Forgiveness and Grace: Joseph's forgiveness of his brothers prefigures the grace offered by Jesus, showing that God's plan includes reconciliation and forgiveness.

Ephesians 4:32 (NIV

"Be kind and compassionate to one another, forgiving each other, just as in Christ God forgave you."

Practical Implications for Believers

1. Trust in God's Plan: Believers can trust in God's sovereignty and faithfulness, knowing that He can use even the most difficult circumstances for good.

2. Embrace Forgiveness: Following the examples of Joseph and Jesus, believers are called to forgive others and seek reconciliation.

3. Proclaim Salvation: Believers are called to share the message of salvation and reconciliation, pointing others to Jesus, the ultimate savior.

2 Corinthians 5:18-20 (NIV):

18 All this is from God, who reconciled us to himself through Christ and gave us the ministry of reconciliation:

19 that God was reconciling the world to himself in Christ, not counting people's sins against them. And he has committed to us the message of reconciliation.

20 We are therefore Christ's ambassadors, as though God were making his appeal through us. We implore you on Christ's behalf: Be reconciled to God.

Conclusion

Joseph's life is a profound foreshadowing of the life and mission of Jesus Christ. Through his suffering, exaltation, and role as the savior of his people, Joseph prefigures the ultimate redemption and reconciliation offered by Jesus. The parallels between Joseph and Jesus highlight the sovereignty of God, the redemptive power of suffering, and the importance of forgiveness and grace. By understanding these connections, believers can deepen their trust in God's plan, embrace the call to forgive, and actively share the message of salvation with the world.

Parallels Between Joseph's Life and Jesus' Life, Death, and Resurrection

Falsely Accused and Suffered

Genesis 39:19-20 (NIV):

19 When his master heard the story his wife told him, saying, "This is how your slave treated me," he burned with anger.

20 Joseph's master took him and put him in prison, the place where the king's prisoners were confined. But while Joseph was there in the prison,

1. Joseph: Falsely accused by Potiphar's wife and unjustly imprisoned.

2. Jesus: Falsely accused by religious leaders and condemned to death.

Mark 14:55-56 (NIV):

55 The chief priests and the whole Sanhedrin were looking for evidence against Jesus so that they could put him to death, but they did not find any.

56 Many testified falsely against him, but their statements did not agree.

Strong's Concordance Insights:

- Accuse (κατηγορέω, katēgoreō, Strong's G2723): To speak against, charge with a crime.

Exalted After Suffering

Genesis 41:39-41 (NIV):

39 Then Pharaoh said to Joseph, "Since God has made all this known to you, there is no one so discerning and wise as you.

40 You shall be in charge of my palace, and all my people are to submit to your orders. Only with respect to the throne will I be greater than you."

41 So Pharaoh said to Joseph, "I hereby put you in charge of the whole land of Egypt."

1. Joseph: After interpreting Pharaoh's dreams, Joseph is exalted to the highest position in Egypt, second only to Pharaoh.

2. Jesus: After His resurrection, Jesus is exalted to the right hand of God, having all authority in heaven and on earth.

Philippians 2:9-11 (NIV):

9 Therefore God exalted him to the highest place and gave him the name that is above every name,

10 that at the name of Jesus every knee should bow, in heaven and on earth and under the earth,

11 and every tongue acknowledge that Jesus Christ is Lord, to the glory of God the Father.

Strong's Concordance Insights:

- Exalt (ὑψόω, hypsoō, Strong's G5312): To lift up, elevate, raise to dignity.

Savior of His People

Genesis 41:56-57 (NIV):

56 When the famine had spread over the whole country, Joseph opened all the storehouses and sold grain to the Egyptians, for the famine was severe throughout Egypt.

57 And all the world came to Egypt to buy grain from Joseph, because the famine was severe everywhere.

1. Joseph: Joseph saves Egypt and the surrounding nations from famine by wisely managing resources during the years of plenty.

2. Jesus: Jesus offers salvation to the whole world, providing spiritual nourishment and eternal life.

John 6:35 (NIV):

Then Jesus declared, "I am the bread of life. Whoever comes to me will never go hungry, and whoever believes in me will never be thirsty."

Strong's Concordance Insights:

- Bread (ἄρτος, artos, Strong's G740): Food, sustenance, that which provides life.

Reconciliation and Forgiveness

Genesis 45:4-8 (NIV):

4 Then Joseph said to his brothers, "Come close to me." When they had done so, he said, "I am your brother Joseph, the one you sold into Egypt!

5 And now, do not be distressed and do not be angry with yourselves for selling me here, because it was to save lives that God sent me ahead of you.

6 For two years now there has been famine in the land, and for the next five years there will be no plowing and reaping.

7 But God sent me ahead of you to preserve for you a remnant on earth and to save your lives by a great deliverance.

8 So then, it was not you who sent me here, but God. He made me father to Pharaoh, lord of his entire household and ruler of all Egypt.

1. Joseph: Joseph forgives his brothers and reconciles with them, recognizing that God used their actions for a greater purpose.

2. Jesus: Jesus offers forgiveness and reconciliation to all who believe in Him, restoring the broken relationship between humanity and God.

Colossians 1:19-20 (NIV):

19 For God was pleased to have all his fullness dwell in him,

20 and through him to reconcile to himself all things, whether things on earth or things in heaven, by making peace through his blood, shed on the cross.

Strong's Concordance Insights:

- Reconcile (ἀποκαταλλάσσω, apokatallassō, Strong's G604): To restore to favor, make peace between parties.

Resurrection Imagery

Genesis 37:31-34 (NIV):

31 Then they got Joseph's robe, slaughtered a goat and dipped the robe in the blood.

32 They took the ornate robe back to their father and said, "We found this. Examine it to see whether it is your son's robe."

33 He recognized it and said, "It is my son's robe! Some ferocious animal has devoured him. Joseph has surely been torn to pieces."

34 Then Jacob tore his clothes, put on sackcloth and mourned for his son many days.

1. Joseph: Joseph's father believes he is dead, but he is later "resurrected" in a sense when he reveals himself to his brothers and is reunited with his family.

2. Jesus: Jesus physically dies on the cross and is resurrected on the third day, confirming His victory over sin and death.

Matthew 28:5-7 (NIV):

5 The angel said to the women, "Do not be afraid, for I know that you are looking for Jesus, who was crucified.

6 He is not here; he has risen, just as he said. Come and see the place where he lay.

7 Then go quickly and tell his disciples: 'He has risen from the dead and is going ahead of you into Galilee. There you will see him.' Now I have told you."

Strong's Concordance Insights:

- Resurrect (ἀνίστημι, anistēmi, Strong's G450): To rise up, to raise from the dead.

Theological Implications

1. God's Sovereignty and Providence: The parallels between Joseph and Jesus highlight God's sovereignty in orchestrating events to bring about His redemptive purposes. Even in suffering and betrayal, God's plan prevails.

2. Redemption Through Suffering: Both Joseph and Jesus demonstrate that suffering can lead to redemption and salvation for many. Their lives teach that God can use even the most painful experiences for good.

3. Forgiveness and Reconciliation: Joseph's forgiveness of his brothers prefigures the grace and forgiveness offered through Jesus. Believers are called to forgive others as they have been forgiven.

Ephesians 4:32 (NIV): "Be kind and compassionate to one another, forgiving each other, just as in Christ God forgave you."

Practical Implications for Believers

1. Trust in God's Plan: Believers can trust in God's sovereign plan, even when faced with suffering and injustice, knowing that He can bring good out of every situation.

Romans 8:28 (NIV): "And we know that in all things God works for the good of those who love him, who have been called according to his purpose."

2. Embrace Forgiveness: Following the examples of Joseph and Jesus, believers are called to forgive others, extending grace and seeking reconciliation.

3. Proclaim the Message of Salvation: Believers are called to share the message of salvation and reconciliation, pointing others to Jesus, the ultimate savior.

2 Corinthians 5:18-20 (NIV):

18 All this is from God, who reconciled us to himself through Christ and gave us the ministry of reconciliation:

19 that God was reconciling the world to himself in Christ, not counting people's sins against them. And he has committed to us the message of reconciliation.

20 We are therefore Christ's ambassadors, as though God were making his appeal through us. We implore you on Christ's behalf: Be reconciled to God.

Conclusion

The life of Joseph serves as a profound foreshadowing of the life, death, and resurrection of Jesus Christ. Through their suffering, exaltation, and roles as saviors, both Joseph and Jesus demonstrate the depth of God's redemptive plan and His sovereign control over history. The parallels between these two figures enrich our understanding of the continuity between the Old and New Testaments and highlight the consistent themes of forgiveness, reconciliation, and salvation. By studying these connections, believers can deepen their faith, embrace the call to forgive, and actively share the message of redemption through Jesus Christ with the world.

CHAPTER 10

JESUS AS THE FULFILLMENT OF THE LAW

The giving of the law and the establishment of the covenant in the Old Testament are foundational to the biblical narrative. These laws and covenants, given to the people of Israel, pointed forward to a greater fulfillment in Jesus Christ. This chapter explores how Jesus fulfills the law and the covenant, highlighting His divine nature and mission. We will examine key biblical passages and provide comprehensive commentary on how Jesus embodies and completes the law's requirements, bringing about the fullness of God's redemptive plan.

The Giving of the Law and Covenant

Genesis 17:1-2 (NIV):

1 When Abram was ninety-nine years old, the Lord appeared to him and said, "I am God Almighty; walk before me faithfully and be blameless.

2 Then I will make my covenant between me and you and will greatly increase your numbers."

Context and Analysis

1. Covenant with Abraham: God establishes a covenant with Abraham, promising to make him a great nation and to bless all nations through his descendants.

2. Sign of the Covenant: The covenant includes specific signs and requirements, such as circumcision, symbolizing the people's commitment to God.

Exodus 19:5-6 (NIV):

5 Now if you obey me fully and keep my covenant, then out of all nations you will be my treasured possession. Although the whole earth is mine,

6 you will be for me a kingdom of priests and a holy nation. These are the words you are to speak to the Israelites.

The Law Given to Moses

1. Mount Sinai: God gives the law to Moses on Mount Sinai, establishing a covenant with the Israelites.

2. Purpose of the Law: The law serves as a guide for righteous living, revealing God's holiness and the standards for His people.

Exodus 20:1-17 (NIV): The Ten Commandments outline the core principles of the law, covering moral, ceremonial, and civil aspects of life.

Strong's Concordance Insights:

- Law (תּוֹרָה, torah, Strong's H8451): Instruction, teaching, a body of legal directives given by God.

- Covenant (בְּרִית, berit, Strong's H1285): An agreement, pact, or treaty between God and humanity.

Jesus as the Fulfillment of the Law

Matthew 5:17 (NIV):

"Do not think that I have come to abolish the Law or the Prophets; I have not come to abolish them but to fulfill them."

Context and Analysis

1. Fulfillment, Not Abolishment: Jesus clarifies that His mission is not to abolish the law but to fulfill its true meaning and purpose.

2. Complete Obedience: Jesus perfectly obeys the law, embodying its principles and bringing it to its intended conclusion.

Romans 8:3-4 (NIV):

3 For what the law was powerless to do because it was weakened by the flesh, God did by sending his own Son in

the likeness of sinful flesh to be a sin offering. And so he condemned sin in the flesh,

4 in order that the righteous requirement of the law might be fully met in us, who do not live according to the flesh but according to the Spirit.

Jesus' Sacrificial Death

1. Sin Offering: Jesus' death on the cross serves as the ultimate sin offering, fulfilling the sacrificial requirements of the law.

2. Righteous Requirement: Through Jesus, the righteous requirements of the law are fully met, enabling believers to live according to the Spirit.

Hebrews 10:1 (NIV):

"The law is only a shadow of the good things that are coming—not the realities themselves. For this reason it can never, by the same sacrifices repeated endlessly year after year, make perfect those who draw near to worship."

The Law as a Shadow

1. Shadow and Reality: The law is a shadow, pointing forward to the realities fulfilled in Christ.

2. Perfection in Christ: The sacrifices of the law could not make people perfect, but Jesus' sacrifice brings true perfection and reconciliation with God.

Strong's Concordance Insights:

- Fulfill (πληρόω, plēroō, Strong's G4137): To make full, to complete, to accomplish.

Jesus' Divinity in Fulfilling the Law

John 1:14 (NIV):

"The Word became flesh and made his dwelling among us. We have seen his glory, the glory of the one and only Son, who came from the Father, full of grace and truth."

Incarnation of the Word

1. Divine Nature: Jesus, as the Word made flesh, reveals the glory of God and embodies divine grace and truth.

2. God's Presence: Jesus' incarnation signifies God's presence among His people, fulfilling the law's requirement for holiness and divine relationship.

Colossians 2:9 (NIV):

"For in Christ all the fullness of the Deity lives in bodily form,"

Fullness of Deity

1. Divine Fullness: Jesus possesses the fullness of deity, making Him uniquely capable of fulfilling the law's demands.

2. Embodiment of God's Nature: In Jesus, the complete nature of God is embodied, affirming His divinity.

Hebrews 1:3 (NIV):

"The Son is the radiance of God's glory and the exact representation of his being, sustaining all things by his powerful word. After he had provided purification for sins, he sat down at the right hand of the Majesty in heaven."

Exact Representation

1. Radiance of Glory: Jesus is the radiance of God's glory, perfectly reflecting God's nature and character.

2. Purification for Sins: Jesus provides purification for sins through His sacrificial death, fulfilling the law's requirements for atonement.

The New Covenant in Jesus

Jeremiah 31:31-34 (NIV):

31 "The days are coming," declares the Lord, "when I will make a new covenant with the people of Israel and with the people of Judah.

32 It will not be like the covenant I made with their ancestors when I took them by the hand to lead them out of Egypt, because they broke my covenant, though I was a husband to them," declares the Lord.

33 "This is the covenant I will make with the people of Israel after that time," declares the Lord. "I will put my law in their minds and write it on their hearts. I will be their God, and they will be my people.

34 No longer will they teach their neighbor, or say to one another, 'Know the Lord,' because they will all know me, from the least of them to the greatest," declares the Lord. "For I will forgive their wickedness and will remember their sins no more."

The Promise of a New Covenant

1. Internalized Law: The new covenant involves the law being written on hearts and minds, signifying an internal transformation.

2. Forgiveness of Sins: This covenant promises the forgiveness of sins, fulfilled in Jesus' sacrificial death and resurrection.

Luke 22:20 (NIV):

"In the same way, after the supper he took the cup, saying, 'This cup is the new covenant in my blood, which is poured out for you.'"

Establishment of the New Covenant

1. Jesus' Blood: The new covenant is established through Jesus' blood, symbolizing the ultimate sacrifice for sin.

2. Divine Fulfillment: Jesus' death and resurrection inaugurate the new covenant, fulfilling the promises of the old covenant.

Practical Implications for Believers

1. Living by the Spirit: Believers are called to live by the Spirit, enabled by Jesus' fulfillment of the law's requirements.

Romans 8:4 (NIV):

"in order that the righteous requirement of the law might be fully met in us, who do not live according to the flesh but according to the Spirit."

2. Internal Transformation: The new covenant emphasizes an internal transformation, where God's law is written on believers' hearts.

2 Corinthians 3:3 (NIV):

"You show that you are a letter from Christ, the result of our ministry, written not with ink but with the Spirit of the living God, not on tablets of stone but on tablets of human hearts."

3. Assurance of Salvation: Believers have assurance of salvation through Jesus' fulfillment of the law, knowing that His sacrifice is sufficient for forgiveness and reconciliation.

Hebrews 10:14 (NIV):

"For by one sacrifice he has made perfect forever those who are being made holy."

Conclusion

Jesus as the fulfillment of the law and the covenant is central to understanding His divine mission and identity.

Through His perfect obedience, sacrificial death, and resurrection, Jesus embodies the law's true purpose and brings it to its intended completion. His fulfillment of the law reveals His divine nature and inaugurates the new covenant, offering forgiveness and internal transformation to all who believe. This profound truth calls believers to live by the Spirit, embrace the internal transformation of the new covenant, and rest in the assurance of salvation provided by Jesus Christ, the ultimate fulfillment of the law.

Jesus as the One Who Perfectly Fulfills the Law

Jesus Christ, in His Sermon on the Mount, made a profound declaration about His relationship to the law: "Do not think that I have come to abolish the Law or the Prophets; I have not come to abolish them but to fulfill them" (Matthew 5:17, NIV). This statement reveals the core of Jesus' mission and His divine purpose. This chapter explores how Jesus fulfills the law, providing an expository Bible study and comprehensive commentary with insights from Strong's Concordance.

The Context of Matthew 5:17

Matthew 5:17 (NIV):

"Do not think that I have come to abolish the Law or the Prophets; I have not come to abolish them but to fulfill them."

Context and Analysis

1. Sermon on the Mount: Jesus delivers this statement during the Sermon on the Mount, a discourse that outlines the principles of His kingdom and the righteousness it demands.

2. Law and Prophets: The phrase "Law or the Prophets" refers to the entirety of the Old Testament scriptures, encompassing the Mosaic Law and the prophetic writings.

3. Fulfill (πληρόω, plēroō, Strong's G4137): To complete, to bring to its intended meaning or purpose.

Strong's Concordance Insights:

- Law (νόμος, nomos, Strong's G3551): The law, especially the Mosaic Law.

- Prophets (προφήτης, prophētēs, Strong's G4396): One who speaks forth by divine inspiration, the Old Testament prophets.

Jesus' Fulfillment of the Law

1. Perfect Obedience to the Law

Matthew 5:18-19 (NIV):

18 For truly I tell you, until heaven and earth disappear, not the smallest letter, not the least stroke of a pen, will by any means disappear from the Law until everything is accomplished.

19 Therefore anyone who sets aside one of the least of these commands and teaches others accordingly will be called least in the kingdom of heaven, but whoever practices and teaches these commands will be called great in the kingdom of heaven.

Expository Study and Commentary:

- Complete Adherence: Jesus emphasizes that every part of the law remains valid until its purpose is accomplished. He fulfills the law by perfectly obeying it in every detail.

- Teaching and Practicing: Jesus not only obeys the law but also teaches its true meaning, correcting misunderstandings and abuses by religious leaders.

Strong's Concordance Insights:

- Accomplished (γίνομαι, ginomai, Strong's G1096): To become, to come into being, indicating the fulfillment or completion of a task or purpose.

2. Fulfillment of Prophetic Predictions

Luke 24:44 (NIV):

He said to them, "This is what I told you while I was still with you: Everything must be fulfilled that is written about me in the Law of Moses, the Prophets and the Psalms."

Expository Study and Commentary:

- Prophetic Fulfillment: Jesus fulfills the messianic prophecies found throughout the Old Testament. His life, death, and resurrection are the realization of these predictions.

- Scriptural Integrity: Jesus' fulfillment of prophecy underscores the reliability and divine inspiration of the scriptures.

Strong's Concordance Insights:

- Fulfilled (πληρόω, plēroō, Strong's G4137): To complete or bring to full measure.

3. Ultimate Sacrifice for Sin

Hebrews 10:11-14 (NIV):

11 Day after day every priest stands and performs his religious duties; again and again he offers the same sacrifices, which can never take away sins.

12 But when this priest had offered for all time one sacrifice for sins, he sat down at the right hand of God,

13 and since that time he waits for his enemies to be made his footstool.

14 For by one sacrifice he has made perfect forever those who are being made holy.

Expository Study and Commentary:

- Final Sacrifice: Jesus' death on the cross is the ultimate and final sacrifice, fulfilling the sacrificial system established in the law.

- Perfect Atonement: His sacrifice achieves what the repetitive sacrifices of the Old Testament could not—complete atonement and purification for sins.

Strong's Concordance Insights:

- Sacrifice (θυσία, thysia, Strong's G2378): An offering, often referring to a sacrificial victim.

- Perfect (τελειόω, teleioō, Strong's G5048): To make complete, to bring to an end goal or purpose.

4. Embodiment of the Law's Intent

Matthew 22:37-40 (NIV):

37 Jesus replied: "'Love the Lord your God with all your heart and with all your soul and with all your mind.'

38 This is the first and greatest commandment.

39 And the second is like it: 'Love your neighbor as yourself.'

40 All the Law and the Prophets hang on these two commandments."

Expository Study and Commentary:

- Law of Love: Jesus distills the law's intent into two overarching commandments: love for God and love for neighbor. He perfectly embodies and teaches this principle.

- Foundation of the Law: These commandments summarize the essence of the law, which Jesus fulfills through His life and teachings.

Strong's Concordance Insights:

- Love (ἀγαπάω, agapaō, Strong's G25): To love, to value, demonstrating the highest form of love and care.

Jesus' Divinity in Fulfilling the Law

1. Incarnation and Divine Nature

John 1:14 (NIV):

"The Word became flesh and made his dwelling among us. We have seen his glory, the glory of the one and only Son, who came from the Father, full of grace and truth."

Expository Study and Commentary:

- Incarnation: Jesus, as the Word made flesh, reveals God's glory and embodies divine truth and grace.

- Divine Presence: His incarnation signifies God's presence among humanity, fulfilling the law's requirement for holiness.

Strong's Concordance Insights:

- Word (λόγος, logos, Strong's G3056): A term denoting the divine expression, often used for Jesus as the preexistent Logos.

- Grace (χάρις, charis, Strong's G5485): Favor, kindness, divine influence upon the heart.

2. Authority Over the Law

Mark 2:27-28 (NIV):

27 Then he said to them, "The Sabbath was made for man, not man for the Sabbath.

28 So the Son of Man is Lord even of the Sabbath."

Expository Study and Commentary:

- Lord of the Sabbath: Jesus asserts His authority over the Sabbath, a central aspect of the law, indicating His divine authority and reinterpretation of the law's intent.

- Redefining Legalism: Jesus challenges legalistic interpretations, emphasizing the law's purpose for human benefit and divine relationship.

Strong's Concordance Insights:

- Lord (κύριος, kyrios, Strong's G2962): Master, one with authority, often used to denote divine lordship.

3. Establishment of the New Covenant

Luke 22:20 (NIV):

"In the same way, after the supper he took the cup, saying, 'This cup is the new covenant in my blood, which is poured out for you.'"

Expository Study and Commentary:

- New Covenant: Jesus inaugurates the new covenant through His sacrificial death, fulfilling the old covenant and establishing a new relationship between God and humanity.

- Blood of the Covenant: His blood signifies the ultimate sacrifice, sealing the new covenant and fulfilling the requirements of the law.

Strong's Concordance Insights:

- Covenant (διαθήκη, diathēkē, Strong's G1242): An agreement, testament, often referring to God's promises to humanity.

Practical Implications for Believers

1. Living by the Spirit

Romans 8:4 (NIV):

"in order that the righteous requirement of the law might be fully met in us, who do not live according to the flesh but according to the Spirit."

Expository Study and Commentary:

- Spirit-Led Life: Believers are called to live by the Spirit, empowered by Jesus' fulfillment of the law's requirements.

- Righteous Living: Through the Spirit, believers fulfill the law's righteous requirements in their daily lives.

Strong's Concordance Insights:

- Spirit (πνεῦμα, pneuma, Strong's G4151): Breath, spirit, often referring to the Holy Spirit.

2. Internal Transformation

2 Corinthians 3:3 (NIV):

"You show that you are a letter from Christ, the result of our ministry, written not with ink but with the Spirit of the living God, not on tablets of stone but on tablets of human hearts."

Expository Study and Commentary:

- Heart Transformation: The new covenant emphasizes internal transformation, where God's law is written on believers' hearts.

- Living Testimony: Believers become living testimonies of Christ's work, reflecting His fulfillment of the law.

Strong's Concordance Insights:

- Heart (καρδία, kardia, Strong's G2588): The inner self, the seat of emotions, thought, and will.

3. Assurance of

Salvation

Hebrews 10:14 (NIV):

"For by one sacrifice he has made perfect forever those who are being made holy."

Expository Study and Commentary:

- Perfect Sacrifice: Jesus' sacrifice provides complete atonement, giving believers assurance of their salvation.

- Ongoing Sanctification: Believers are made holy through Jesus' perfect fulfillment of the law, ensuring their eternal security.

Strong's Concordance Insights:

- Holy (ἁγιάζω, hagiazō, Strong's G37): To make holy, to sanctify, to set apart for God's purposes.

Conclusion

Jesus' declaration that He came not to abolish the law but to fulfill it reveals the depth of His divine mission and identity. Through His perfect obedience, sacrificial death, and resurrection, Jesus embodies the law's true purpose and brings it to its intended completion. His fulfillment of the law highlights His divine nature and establishes the new covenant, offering forgiveness and internal transformation to all who believe. This profound truth calls believers to live by the Spirit, embrace the internal transformation of the new covenant, and rest in the assurance of salvation provided by Jesus Christ, the ultimate fulfillment of the law.

The Continuity of God's Plan from Genesis to the New Testament

The Bible, though composed of various books written over centuries, presents a unified narrative that reveals the continuity of God's redemptive plan from Genesis to the New Testament. This chapter explores how God's plan unfolds through the scriptures, culminating in the life, death, and resurrection of Jesus Christ. By examining key themes and events from Genesis through to the New Testament, we can see the coherence of God's purpose and His unwavering commitment to redeeming humanity.

The Foundation in Genesis

Genesis 1:1 (NIV):

"In the beginning God created the heavens and the earth."

The Creation

1. Divine Creation: The Bible begins with the creation narrative, establishing God as the sovereign creator of all things.

2. Humanity's Role: Humans are created in God's image, intended to have dominion over creation and to live in relationship with God.

Genesis 3:15 (NIV):

"And I will put enmity between you and the woman, and between your offspring and hers; he will crush your head, and you will strike his heel."

The Fall and the First Promise

1. The Fall: Humanity's disobedience introduces sin and death into the world, breaking the perfect relationship between God and humans.

2. Protoevangelium: The first promise of redemption is given, foretelling the defeat of the serpent (Satan) by the offspring of the woman, a foreshadowing of Jesus' victory over sin.

Genesis 12:1-3 (NIV):

1 The Lord had said to Abram, "Go from your country, your people and your father's household to the land I will show you.

2 "I will make you into a great nation, and I will bless you; I will make your name great, and you will be a blessing.

3 I will bless those who bless you, and whoever curses you I will curse; and all peoples on earth will be blessed through you."

The Covenant with Abraham

1. Calling of Abraham: God calls Abraham to leave his homeland and promises to make him a great nation.

2. Blessing to All Nations: God's promise to Abraham includes blessings for all nations, indicating the global scope of His redemptive plan.

The Development of God's Plan

Exodus 3:7-10 (NIV):

7 The Lord said, "I have indeed seen the misery of my people in Egypt. I have heard them crying out because of their slave drivers, and I am concerned about their suffering.

8 So I have come down to rescue them from the hand of the Egyptians and to bring them up out of that land into a good and spacious land, a land flowing with milk and honey— the home of the Canaanites, Hittites, Amorites, Perizzites, Hivites and Jebusites.

9 And now the cry of the Israelites has reached me, and I have seen the way the Egyptians are oppressing them.

10 So now, go. I am sending you to Pharaoh to bring my people the Israelites out of Egypt."

The Exodus and the Mosaic Covenant

1. Deliverance from Egypt: God's rescue of the Israelites from Egyptian slavery is a pivotal event, demonstrating His power and faithfulness.

2. The Law: At Mount Sinai, God gives the law to Moses, establishing a covenant that sets Israel apart as His chosen people.

Exodus 19:5-6 (NIV):

5 Now if you obey me fully and keep my covenant, then out of all nations you will be my treasured possession. Although the whole earth is mine,

6 you will be for me a kingdom of priests and a holy nation.' These are the words you are to speak to the Israelites."

The Purpose of the Law

1. Holy Nation: The law is given to shape Israel into a kingdom of priests and a holy nation, demonstrating God's righteousness to the world.

2. Foreshadowing Christ: The sacrificial system and various laws foreshadow the ultimate sacrifice of Jesus and the establishment of the new covenant.

Isaiah 53:5 (NIV):

"But he was pierced for our transgressions, he was crushed for our iniquities; the punishment that brought us peace was on him, and by his wounds we are healed."

Prophetic Promises

1. Suffering Servant: The prophets, especially Isaiah, foretell the coming of a suffering servant who will bear the sins of many, pointing directly to Jesus' atoning work.

2. New Covenant: Jeremiah and Ezekiel prophesy about a new covenant where God's law will be written on hearts, indicating a deeper, more personal relationship with God.

Jeremiah 31:31-34 (NIV):

31 "The days are coming," declares the Lord, "when I will make a new covenant with the people of Israel and with the people of Judah.

32 It will not be like the covenant I made with their ancestors when I took them by the hand to lead them out of

Egypt, because they broke my covenant, though I was a husband to them," declares the Lord.

33 "This is the covenant I will make with the people of Israel after that time," declares the Lord. "I will put my law in their minds and write it on their hearts. I will be their God, and they will be my people.

34 No longer will they teach their neighbor, or say to one another, 'Know the Lord,' because they will all know me, from the least of them to the greatest," declares the Lord. "For I will forgive their wickedness and will remember their sins no more."

Fulfillment in Jesus Christ

Matthew 5:17 (NIV):

"Do not think that I have come to abolish the Law or the Prophets; I have not come to abolish them but to fulfill them."

Jesus as the Fulfillment

1. Perfect Fulfillment: Jesus fulfills the law and the prophets by embodying their true intent and purpose, living a sinless life, and completing the sacrificial system.

2. New Covenant Establishment: His death and resurrection establish the new covenant, fulfilling the promises of the Old Testament.

Luke 24:44 (NIV):

He said to them, "This is what I told you while I was still with you: Everything must be fulfilled that is written about me in the Law of Moses, the Prophets and the Psalms."

Resurrection and Fulfillment

1. Scriptural Fulfillment: Jesus' resurrection is the culmination of the Old Testament prophecies, confirming His identity as the Messiah and the fulfillment of God's redemptive plan.

2. Opening of the Scriptures: After His resurrection, Jesus opens the minds of His disciples to understand how the scriptures point to Him.

Romans 8:3-4 (NIV):

3 For what the law was powerless to do because it was weakened by the flesh, God did by sending his own Son in the likeness of sinful flesh to be a sin offering. And so he condemned sin in the flesh,

4 in order that the righteous requirement of the law might be fully met in us, who do not live according to the flesh but according to the Spirit.

The Role of Jesus' Sacrifice

1. Sin Offering: Jesus' death as a sin offering fulfills the sacrificial requirements of the law, providing a once-for-all atonement for sin.

2. Righteous Requirement: Through Jesus, the righteous requirements of the law are fully met in believers who live by the Spirit.

Continuity and Consummation

Revelation 21:1-4 (NIV):

1 Then I saw "a new heaven and a new earth," for the first heaven and the first earth had passed away, and there was no longer any sea.

2 I saw the Holy City, the new Jerusalem, coming down out of heaven from God, prepared as a bride beautifully dressed for her husband.

3 And I heard a loud voice from the throne saying, "Look! God's dwelling place is now among the people, and he will dwell with them. They will be his people, and God himself will be with them and be their God.

4 'He will wipe every tear from their eyes. There will be no more death' or mourning or crying or pain, for the old order of things has passed away."

The New Creation

1. Eternal Consummation: The continuity of God's plan is ultimately consummated in the new creation, where God dwells with His people eternally.

2. Fulfillment of Promises: All the promises from Genesis through the New Testament find their final fulfillment in the new heaven and new earth.

Theological Implications

1. God's Faithfulness: The continuity of God's plan from Genesis to the New Testament demonstrates His unwavering faithfulness and commitment to His promises.

2. Christ-Centered Narrative: The entire biblical narrative centers on Jesus Christ, from the protoevangelium in Genesis to the fulfillment of the new creation in Revelation.

3. Redemptive Plan: God's redemptive plan unfolds progressively, revealing His purpose to redeem humanity and restore creation through Jesus.

Practical Implications for Believers

1. Trust in God's Plan: Believers can trust in God's sovereign plan, knowing that He has faithfully worked through history to bring about redemption.

2. Live by the Spirit: In light of Jesus' fulfillment of the law, believers are called to live by the Spirit, embodying the righteousness of the new covenant.

3. Hope in the Future: The promise of the new creation gives believers hope and assurance of God's ultimate victory over sin and death.

2 Peter

3:13 (NIV):

"But in keeping with his promise we are looking forward to a new heaven and a new earth, where righteousness dwells."

Conclusion

The continuity of God's plan from Genesis to the New Testament reveals a coherent and purposeful narrative that culminates in Jesus Christ. Through His life, death, and resurrection, Jesus fulfills the law and the prophets, establishing the new covenant and securing eternal redemption for humanity. This overarching story of God's redemptive work demonstrates His faithfulness, the centrality of Christ, and the hope of a restored creation. Believers are called to trust in this divine plan, live by the Spirit, and look forward with hope to the consummation of all things in the new creation.

CHAPTER 11

JESUS' ROLE IN BRINGING ABOUT THE NEW CREATION

The Bible reveals that Jesus Christ plays a central role in bringing about the new creation, a concept that embodies both personal transformation and the ultimate renewal of all things. Key scriptures such as 2 Corinthians 5:17 and Revelation 21:1-5 illuminate this profound truth. This chapter explores Jesus' role in the new creation, emphasizing both the individual transformation of believers and the eschatological promise of a new heaven and new earth.

New Creation in Believers

2 Corinthians 5:17 (NIV):

"Therefore, if anyone is in Christ, the new creation has come: The old has gone, the new is here!"

Context and Analysis

1. In Christ: The phrase "in Christ" signifies a profound spiritual union with Jesus, where believers are intimately connected to Him.

2. New Creation: This term denotes a radical transformation, signifying the beginning of a new existence marked by spiritual renewal and the indwelling of the Holy Spirit.

3. Old and New: The old refers to the former way of life dominated by sin, while the new represents a life transformed by the grace and power of Christ.

Strong's Concordance Insights:

- New (καινός, kainos, Strong's G2537): New in quality, fresh, unprecedented.

- Creation (κτίσις, ktisis, Strong's G2937): Act of creating, the result of a creative act, creation.

Expository Study and Commentary:

1. Transformation through Christ: Believers become new creations through their relationship with Christ, signifying a fundamental change in identity and purpose.

2. Indwelling Spirit: The Holy Spirit's presence in believers facilitates this transformation, enabling them to live in accordance with God's will.

3. Redemption and Renewal: This new creation is part of God's redemptive plan, illustrating His desire to restore and renew individuals.

Ephesians 4:22-24 (NIV):

22 You were taught, with regard to your former way of life, to put off your old self, which is being corrupted by its deceitful desires;

23 to be made new in the attitude of your minds;

24 and to put on the new self, created to be like God in true righteousness and holiness.

The New Self

1. Putting Off the Old Self: Believers are called to renounce their former sinful behaviors and attitudes.

2. Renewed Minds: Transformation involves a renewal of the mind, aligning thoughts and attitudes with God's truth.

3. New Self: The new self is characterized by righteousness and holiness, reflecting God's nature.

Romans 6:4 (NIV):

"We were therefore buried with him through baptism into death in order that, just as Christ was raised from the dead through the glory of the Father, we too may live a new life."

New Life in Christ

1. Union with Christ in Baptism: Baptism symbolizes the believer's identification with Christ's death, burial, and resurrection.

2. Living a New Life: Believers are empowered to live new lives that reflect the transformative power of Christ's resurrection.

The Eschatological New Creation

Revelation 21:1-5 (NIV):

1 Then I saw "a new heaven and a new earth," for the first heaven and the first earth had passed away, and there was no longer any sea.

2 I saw the Holy City, the new Jerusalem, coming down out of heaven from God, prepared as a bride beautifully dressed for her husband.

3 And I heard a loud voice from the throne saying, "Look! God's dwelling place is now among the people, and he will dwell with them. They will be his people, and God himself will be with them and be their God.

4 'He will wipe every tear from their eyes. There will be no more death' or mourning or crying or pain, for the old order of things has passed away."

5 He who was seated on the throne said, "I am making everything new!" Then he said, "Write this down, for these words are trustworthy and true."

Context and Analysis

1. New Heaven and New Earth: This vision represents the ultimate renewal of creation, where the old order marred by sin and decay is replaced by a new, perfect creation.

2. New Jerusalem: The Holy City symbolizes the redeemed community of believers, beautifully prepared and united with God.

3. God's Dwelling Place: The new creation culminates in the intimate presence of God with His people, signifying restored fellowship and eternal communion.

Strong's Concordance Insights:

- New (καινός, kainos, Strong's G2537): New in quality, fresh, unprecedented.

- Earth (γῆ, gē, Strong's G1093): The physical earth, land, ground.

- Heaven (οὐρανός, ouranos, Strong's G3772): The sky, the abode of God.

Expository Study and Commentary:

1. Ultimate Renewal: The new heaven and new earth represent the consummation of God's redemptive plan, where creation is restored to its intended perfection.

2. Presence of God: The promise of God dwelling among His people fulfills the covenantal promises throughout

scripture, highlighting the intimate relationship between God and humanity.

3. End of Suffering: The eradication of death, mourning, crying, and pain signifies the complete victory over sin and its consequences, bringing eternal joy and peace.

2 Peter 3:13 (NIV):

"But in keeping with his promise we are looking forward to a new heaven and a new earth, where righteousness dwells."

Hope of Righteousness

1. Promise of Renewal: Believers are encouraged to look forward to the new creation, where righteousness will dwell permanently.

2. Assurance of Fulfillment: God's promise of a new creation is trustworthy and true, providing hope and motivation for holy living.

Romans 8:18-21 (NIV):

18 I consider that our present sufferings are not worth comparing with the glory that will be revealed in us.

19 For the creation waits in eager expectation for the children of God to be revealed.

20 For the creation was subjected to frustration, not by its own choice, but by the will of the one who subjected it, in hope

21 that the creation itself will be liberated from its bondage to decay and brought into the freedom and glory of the children of God.

Liberation of Creation

1. Present Sufferings vs. Future Glory: The sufferings of the present are insignificant compared to the future glory that will be revealed.

2. Eager Expectation: All of creation eagerly anticipates the fulfillment of God's redemptive plan, longing for liberation from decay.

3. Children of God Revealed: The final redemption includes the full revelation of believers as God's children, sharing in His glory.

Jesus' Role in the New Creation

1. Agent of Creation and Re-Creation

Colossians 1:16-17 (NIV):

16 For in him all things were created: things in heaven and on earth, visible and invisible, whether thrones or powers or rulers or authorities; all things have been created through him and for him.

17 He is before all things, and in him all things hold together.

Expository Study and Commentary:

- Creator of All Things: Jesus is the agent through whom all things were created, emphasizing His divine authority and power.

- Sustainer of Creation: Jesus holds all things together, ensuring the stability and coherence of creation.

- Re-Creation: As the agent of the new creation, Jesus initiates and brings to completion the renewal of all things, fulfilling God's redemptive purposes.

Strong's Concordance Insights:

- Created (κτίζω, ktizō, Strong's G2936): To create, to make.

- Hold Together (συνίστημι, synistēmi, Strong's G4921): To set together, to unite, to sustain.

2. Firstborn from the Dead

Revelation 1:5 (NIV):

"...and from Jesus Christ, who is the faithful witness, the firstborn from the dead, and the ruler of the kings of the earth. To him who loves us and has freed us from our sins by his blood,"

Expository Study and Commentary:

- Firstborn from the Dead: Jesus' resurrection is the first instance of the new creation, guaranteeing the future resurrection and renewal of all believers.

- Ruler and Redeemer: Jesus' authority as the ruler of the kings of the earth and His role as redeemer through His blood highlight His central role in the new creation.

Strong's Concordance Insights:

- Firstborn (πρωτότοκος, prōtotokos, Strong's G4416): First in rank, preeminent, the first to rise from the dead in a new, glorified body.

3. Restoration of All Things

Acts 3:21 (NIV):

"Heaven must receive him until the time comes for God to restore everything, as he promised long ago through his holy prophets."

Expository Study and Commentary:

- Restoration: Jesus will return to restore all things, fulfilling the prophecies and promises of God.

- Prophetic Fulfillment: The restoration of all things is part of God's long-standing promise, showing the continuity and consistency of His redemptive plan.

Strong's Concordance Insights:

- Restore (ἀποκατάστασις, ap

okatastasis, Strong's G605): Reconstitution, restoration to an original or improved state.

Practical Implications for Believers

1. Living as New Creations

Ephesians 2:10 (NIV):

"For we are God's handiwork, created in Christ Jesus to do good works, which God prepared in advance for us to do."

Expository Study and Commentary:

- God's Handiwork: Believers are God's workmanship, created anew in Christ to fulfill His purposes.

- Good Works: Living as new creations involves engaging in good works, reflecting God's character and advancing His kingdom.

Strong's Concordance Insights:

- Handiwork (ποίημα, poiēma, Strong's G4161): That which is made, a work or creation.

2. Hope and Anticipation

Titus 2:13 (NIV):

"while we wait for the blessed hope—the appearing of the glory of our great God and Savior, Jesus Christ,"

Expository Study and Commentary:

- Blessed Hope: Believers live in anticipation of Christ's return and the consummation of the new creation.

- Active Waiting: This hope motivates believers to live righteously and participate in God's redemptive work in the world.

Strong's Concordance Insights:

- Hope (ἐλπίς, elpis, Strong's G1680): Expectation, trust, confident anticipation.

3. Proclaiming the New Creation

2 Corinthians 5:20 (NIV):

"We are therefore Christ's ambassadors, as though God were making his appeal through us. We implore you on Christ's behalf: Be reconciled to God."

Expository Study and Commentary:

- Ambassadors for Christ: Believers are called to represent Christ and proclaim the message of reconciliation and new creation.

- Reconciliation: The message of the new creation includes the call for all to be reconciled to God through Jesus Christ.

Strong's Concordance Insights:

- Ambassador (πρεσβεύω, presbeuō, Strong's G4243): To act as a representative, to be an ambassador.

Jesus Christ plays a central role in bringing about the new creation, both in the personal transformation of believers and the ultimate renewal of all things. Through His life, death, and resurrection, Jesus initiates and guarantees the fulfillment of God's redemptive plan. The new creation encompasses individual renewal, communal restoration, and the eschatological promise of a new heaven and new earth.

Believers are called to live as new creations, motivated by hope and empowered by the Spirit to proclaim the message of reconciliation and participate in God's ongoing work of renewal. The continuity and consummation of God's plan highlight His faithfulness, the centrality of Christ, and the hope of eternal fellowship with God in the new creation.

The Hope of Restoration and Redemption Through Jesus

The message of the Bible is fundamentally one of hope, restoration, and redemption, centered in the person and work of Jesus Christ. This chapter explores the multifaceted aspects of Jesus' role in bringing restorative justice, ending the curse of the law, fulfilling retributive justice, and providing the only path to salvation and eternal hope. By examining key biblical passages and theological principles, we can understand why Jesus is the ultimate source of hope for humanity.

Jesus as Restorative Justice

Luke 4:18-19 (NIV):

18 "The Spirit of the Lord is on me,

because he has anointed me

to proclaim good news to the poor.

He has sent me to proclaim freedom for the prisoners

and recovery of sight for the blind,

to set the oppressed free,

19   to proclaim the year of the Lord's favor."

Restorative Mission

1. Anointed to Restore: Jesus declares His mission using Isaiah's prophecy, emphasizing His role in bringing good news, freedom, healing, and liberation.

2. Focus on Restoration: His ministry focuses on restoring individuals and communities, addressing physical, spiritual, and social brokenness.

Strong's Concordance Insights:

- Freedom (ἄφεσις, aphesis, Strong's G859): Release, forgiveness, liberty.

- Oppressed (τεθραυσμένους, tethrausmenous, Strong's G2352): Broken, crushed, shattered.

John 10:10 (NIV):

"The thief comes only to steal and kill and destroy; I have come that they may have life, and have it to the full."

Abundant Life

1. Life to the Full: Jesus offers not just life, but abundant life, characterized by spiritual fullness and restoration.

2. Restorative Justice: His life and teachings emphasize restorative justice—restoring individuals to wholeness and right relationship with God and others.

Ending the Curse of the Law

Galatians 3:13 (NIV):

"Christ redeemed us from the curse of the law by becoming a curse for us, for it is written: 'Cursed is everyone who is hung on a pole.'"

Redemption from the Curse

1. Becoming a Curse: Jesus takes upon Himself the curse of the law by dying on the cross, thereby redeeming humanity from its consequences.

2. Fulfillment of the Law: His sacrificial death fulfills the law's demands, bringing an end to its curse for those who believe in Him.

Strong's Concordance Insights:

- Redeem (ἐξαγοράζω, exagorazō, Strong's G1805): To buy back, to ransom.

- Curse (κατάρα, katara, Strong's G2671): An imprecation, a curse.

Romans 8:1-2 (NIV):

1 Therefore, there is now no condemnation for those who are in Christ Jesus,

2 because through Christ Jesus the law of the Spirit who gives life has set you free from the law of sin and death.

Freedom from Condemnation

1. No Condemnation: Believers are no longer under condemnation because Jesus has set them free from the law of sin and death.

2. Spirit of Life: The law of the Spirit brings life, in contrast to the law of sin and death, which brought condemnation.

Retributive Justice and Jesus' Sacrifice

Isaiah 53:5-6 (NIV):

5 But he was pierced for our transgressions,
    he was crushed for our iniquities;
the punishment that brought us peace was on him,
    and by his wounds we are healed.
6 We all, like sheep, have gone astray,
    each of us has turned to our own way;
and the Lord has laid on him
    the iniquity of us all.

Atoning Sacrifice

1. Punishment for Peace: Jesus' suffering and death fulfill the demands of retributive justice, taking the punishment for sin upon Himself.

2. Substitutionary Atonement: By bearing the iniquities of humanity, Jesus provides a way for peace and healing.

Strong's Concordance Insights:

- Pierced (מְחֹלָל, meholal, Strong's H2490): Wounded, perforated.

- Iniquities (עָוֹן, avon, Strong's H5771): Guilt, punishment for iniquity.

Romans 3:25-26 (NIV):

25 God presented Christ as a sacrifice of atonement, through the shedding of his blood—to be received by faith. He did this to demonstrate his righteousness, because in his forbearance he had left the sins committed beforehand unpunished—

26 he did it to demonstrate his righteousness at the present time, so as to be just and the one who justifies those who have faith in Jesus.

Justice and Justification

1. Sacrifice of Atonement: Jesus is presented as a sacrifice of atonement, satisfying the requirements of God's justice.

2. God's Righteousness: This act demonstrates God's righteousness, being both just and the justifier of those who have faith in Jesus.

Jesus as the Only Savior

Acts 4:12 (NIV):

"Salvation is found in no one else, for there is no other name under heaven given to mankind by which we must be saved."

Exclusivity of Salvation

1. No Other Name: Jesus is the only one through whom salvation is available, emphasizing the exclusivity of His role as Savior.

2. Divine Authority: His name carries divine authority and power, providing the means for salvation.

John 14:6 (NIV):

"Jesus answered, 'I am the way and the truth and the life. No one comes to the Father except through me.'"

Way, Truth, and Life

1. The Way: Jesus is the path to the Father, the only way to reconciliation with God.

2. The Truth: He embodies the ultimate truth, revealing God's nature and will.

3. The Life: Jesus imparts eternal life, transforming the present and future realities of believers.

1 Timothy 2:5-6 (NIV):

5 For there is one God and one mediator between God and mankind, the man Christ Jesus,

6 who gave himself as a ransom for all people. This has now been witnessed to at the proper time.

Mediator and Ransom

1. One Mediator: Jesus is the sole mediator between God and humanity, facilitating reconciliation and access to God.

2. Ransom for All: His self-sacrifice serves as a ransom, paying the price for sin and providing redemption.

Strong's Concordance Insights:

- Mediator (μεσίτης, mesitēs, Strong's G3316): One who intervenes between two parties, especially for the purpose of reconciliation.

- Ransom (ἀντίλυτρον, antilytron, Strong's G487): A substitute ransom, the price paid for release.

Jesus as the Only Hope

Colossians 1:27 (NIV):

"To them God has chosen to make known among the Gentiles the glorious riches of this mystery, which is Christ in you, the hope of glory."

Hope of Glory

1. Christ in You: The indwelling presence of Christ is the hope of future glory for believers.

2. Glorious Riches: This hope encompasses the richness of God's grace and the promise of eternal life.

1 Peter 1:3-4 (NIV):

3 Praise be to the God and Father of our Lord Jesus Christ! In his great mercy he has given us new birth into a living hope through the resurrection of Jesus Christ from the dead,

4 and into an inheritance that can never perish, spoil or fade. This inheritance is kept in heaven for you,

Living Hope

1. New Birth: Through Jesus' resurrection, believers are given a new birth into a living hope.

2. Eternal Inheritance: This hope includes an imperishable, undefiled, and unfading inheritance reserved in heaven.

Hebrews 6:19-20 (NIV):

19 We have this hope as an anchor for the soul, firm and secure. It enters the inner sanctuary behind the curtain,

20 where our forerunner, Jesus, has entered on our behalf. He has become a high priest forever, in the order of Melchizedek.

Anchor for the Soul

1. Firm and Secure: The hope in Jesus serves as a steadfast anchor for believers, providing stability and security.

2. High Priest: Jesus, as the eternal high priest, ensures continuous access to God and ongoing intercession.

Strong's Concordance Insights:

- Hope (ἐλπίς, elpis, Strong's G1680): Expectation, trust, confident anticipation.

- Anchor (ἄγκυρα, ankura, Strong's G45): A device to keep a vessel from drifting, symbolizing stability.

Practical Implications for Believers

1. Living Out Restorative Justice

Micah 6:8 (NIV):

"He has shown you, O mortal, what is good. And what does the Lord require of you? To act justly and to love mercy and to walk humbly with your God."

Expository Study and Commentary:

- Act Justly: Believers are called to pursue justice, reflecting Jesus' restorative work in their lives and

   communities.

- Love Mercy: Compassion and mercy are integral to living out restorative justice.

- Walk Humbly: A humble walk with God aligns believers with His purposes and character.

2. Assurance of No Condemnation

Romans 8:1 (NIV):

"Therefore, there is now no condemnation for those who are in Christ Jesus,"

Expository Study and Commentary:

- Freedom in Christ: Believers can live confidently, knowing they are free from condemnation through Jesus.

- New Identity: Embracing the identity of being in Christ fosters a life of freedom and purpose.

3. Hope-Filled Living

1 Thessalonians 4:13-14 (NIV):

13 Brothers and sisters, we do not want you to be uninformed about those who sleep in death, so that you do not grieve like the rest of mankind, who have no hope.

14 For we believe that Jesus died and rose again, and so we believe that God will bring with Jesus those who have fallen asleep in him.

Expository Study and Commentary:

- Hope in Resurrection: Believers have hope in the resurrection, providing comfort and assurance in the face of death.

- Eternal Perspective: This hope influences how believers live, encouraging them to remain steadfast in faith and love.

Conclusion

Jesus Christ embodies the hope of restoration and redemption, fulfilling God's plan through His life, death, and resurrection. As the source of restorative justice, He ends the curse of the law and satisfies retributive justice through His atoning sacrifice. Jesus stands as the only Savior and mediator, providing the sole path to salvation and eternal hope. Believers are called to live out this hope through just and merciful actions, confident in their freedom from condemnation and anchored by the promise of eternal life. Jesus, the hope of glory, ensures that the redemption and restoration He began will be consummated in the new creation, where righteousness, peace, and joy will reign forever.

CHAPTER 12

CONCLUSION

As we conclude this comprehensive exploration of Jesus Christ's divinity, His fulfillment of the law, and His role in God's redemptive plan, it is essential to reflect on the key themes and insights discussed throughout the book. This chapter provides a summary of the critical points covered, emphasizing how each aspect contributes to a deeper understanding of Jesus and His mission.

Key Points Summary

Jesus' Divine Nature and Mission

1. The Divinity of Jesus

- Jesus is revealed as the Son of God, co-equal and co-eternal with the Father and the Holy Spirit. His divine nature is affirmed through His actions, teachings, and fulfillment of Old Testament prophecies.

- Key Scriptures: John 1:1-3, Colossians 1:15-17, Hebrews 1:3.

2. Jesus and the "I Am" Statements

- Jesus' "I Am" statements in the New Testament echo the divine name revealed to Moses in Exodus 3:14, affirming His eternal existence and divinity.

- Key Scriptures: John 8:58, John 14:6, Exodus 3:14.

Jesus in the Old Testament

3. Jesus' Pre-existence and Creation

- Jesus is not only the fulfillment of the law but also the agent of creation. His existence before His earthly life is highlighted in both the Old and New Testaments.

- Key Scriptures: Genesis 1:1, John 1:1-3, Colossians 1:16.

4. Joseph as a Type of Christ

- The life of Joseph in Genesis prefigures Jesus' life, death, and resurrection. Joseph's suffering, betrayal, and eventual exaltation mirror Jesus' redemptive mission.

- Key Scriptures: Genesis 37-50, Acts 7:9-10, Matthew 26:14-15.

5. Prophetic Fulfillment in Jesus

- Prophecies throughout the Old Testament point to the coming of Jesus as the Messiah, who fulfills God's promises of redemption.

- Key Scriptures: Isaiah 53, Jeremiah 31:31-34, Luke 24:44.

Jesus and the Law

6. Fulfillment of the Law

- Jesus declares that He came not to abolish the law but to fulfill it, completing its purpose and embodying its true meaning.

- Key Scriptures: Matthew 5:17, Romans 8:3-4, Hebrews 10:1.

7. Redemption from the Curse of the Law

- By becoming a curse for us, Jesus redeems humanity from the curse of the law, offering freedom and life through His sacrifice.

- Key Scriptures: Galatians 3:13, Romans 8:1-2, Hebrews 9:15.

The New Creation and Redemption

8. New Creation in Christ

- Believers are made new creations in Christ, experiencing a radical transformation that reflects God's redemptive work.

- Key Scriptures: 2 Corinthians 5:17, Ephesians 4:22-24, Romans 6:4.

9. Eschatological Hope

- The ultimate renewal of all things is promised through Jesus, culminating in a new heaven and a new earth where God dwells with His people.

- Key Scriptures: Revelation 21:1-5, 2 Peter 3:13, Romans 8:18-21.

Jesus as the Only Savior and Hope

10. Exclusive Path to Salvation

- Jesus is the only mediator between God and humanity, the sole source of salvation and eternal life.

- Key Scriptures: John 14:6, Acts 4:12, 1 Timothy 2:5-6.

11. Living Hope Through Jesus

- Jesus provides a living hope through His resurrection, ensuring an eternal inheritance for believers.

- Key Scriptures: 1 Peter 1:3-4, Hebrews 6:19-20, Colossians 1:27.

Practical Implications for Believers

12. Restorative Justice and Living by the Spirit

- Believers are called to live out the principles of restorative justice, reflecting Jesus' mission and embodying the righteousness of the new covenant.

- Key Scriptures: Micah 6:8, Romans 8:4, 2 Corinthians 5:20.

13. Hope-Filled Living and Assurance of Salvation

- The assurance of salvation and the hope of resurrection empower believers to live confidently and purposefully, anchored in the promises of God.

- Key Scriptures: Romans 8:1, 1 Thessalonians 4:13-14, Titus 2:13.

Conclusion

Throughout this book, we have examined the profound and multifaceted role of Jesus Christ in God's redemptive plan. From His divine nature and fulfillment of the law to His pivotal role in the new creation and ultimate hope for humanity, Jesus stands at the center of God's narrative of salvation. By understanding these key points, believers can deepen their faith, live out their calling with purpose, and remain anchored in the hope that Jesus provides. As we continue to study and reflect on these truths, may we be continually transformed by the grace and power of Jesus Christ, our Lord and Savior.

The Significance of Understanding Jesus' Divinity and His Connection to Genesis

Understanding Jesus' divinity and His connection to the book of Genesis is crucial for comprehending the entirety of the biblical narrative and God's redemptive plan. The foundation laid in Genesis provides the context for Jesus' role as Creator, Redeemer, and Fulfillment of God's promises.

This chapter explores the significance of these connections, drawing on key biblical teachings and verses to highlight the profound implications for faith and theology.

Jesus' Divinity: The Foundation of Christian Faith

1. The Eternal Word

John 1:1-3 (NIV):

1 In the beginning was the Word, and the Word was with God, and the Word was God.

2 He was with God in the beginning.

3 Through him all things were made; without him nothing was made that has been made.

Explanation:

- Eternal Existence: Jesus, the Word, existed with God from the beginning, emphasizing His eternal nature and divinity.

- Agent of Creation: Jesus is not only the divine Word but also the agent through whom all things were created. This underscores His active role in the creation narrative found in Genesis.

2. The Image of the Invisible God

Colossians 1:15-17 (NIV):

15 The Son is the image of the invisible God, the firstborn over all creation.

16 For in him all things were created: things in heaven and on earth, visible and invisible, whether thrones or powers or rulers or authorities; all things have been created through him and for him.

17 He is before all things, and in him all things hold together.

Explanation:

- Image of God: Jesus perfectly reflects God's nature and essence, making the invisible God visible to humanity.

- Preeminence in Creation: As the firstborn over all creation, Jesus holds a position of supremacy, indicating His authority and divinity. Everything in existence is created through Him and for Him, aligning with the creation account in Genesis.

Jesus in Genesis: The Foundations of Redemption

1. The Promised Seed

Genesis 3:15 (NIV):

And I will put enmity between you and the woman, and between your offspring and hers; he will crush your head, and you will strike his heel.

Explanation:

- Protoevangelium: This verse, known as the protoevangelium, is the first gospel proclamation, foreshadowing Jesus' victory over Satan and sin. It sets the stage for the unfolding of God's redemptive plan through Jesus, the promised seed.

2. The Covenant with Abraham

Genesis 12:1-3 (NIV):

1 The Lord had said to Abram, "Go from your country, your people and your father's household to the land I will show you.

2 "I will make you into a great nation, and I will bless you; I will make your name great, and you will be a blessing.

3 I will bless those who bless you, and whoever curses you I will curse; and all peoples on earth will be blessed through you."

Explanation:

- Blessing to All Nations: The promise made to Abraham finds its ultimate fulfillment in Jesus Christ, through whom all nations are blessed. Jesus is the descendant through whom God's promise of blessing and redemption extends to all humanity.

Galatians 3:16 (NIV):

The promises were spoken to Abraham and to his seed. Scripture does not say "and to seeds," meaning many people, but "and to your seed," meaning one person, who is Christ.

Explanation:

- Christ as the Seed: Paul clarifies that the promise was ultimately about Jesus, the singular seed of Abraham, emphasizing the continuity of God's redemptive plan from Genesis through to the New Testament.

3. Melchizedek: A Foreshadowing of Christ

Genesis 14:18-20 (NIV):

18 Then Melchizedek king of Salem brought out bread and wine. He was priest of God Most High,

19 and he blessed Abram, saying, "Blessed be Abram by God Most High, Creator of heaven and earth.

20 And praise be to God Most High, who delivered your enemies into your hand." Then Abram gave him a tenth of everything.

Explanation:

- Priest and King: Melchizedek, a mysterious figure who is both priest and king, prefigures Christ, who holds the dual role of our eternal High Priest and King of Kings.

- Eternal Priesthood: The New Testament book of Hebrews explains that Jesus is a priest in the order of Melchizedek, highlighting His eternal and unique priesthood.

Hebrews 7:1-3 (NIV):

1 This Melchizedek was king of Salem and priest of God Most High. He met Abraham returning from the defeat of the kings and blessed him,

2 and Abraham gave him a tenth of everything. First, the name Melchizedek means "king of righteousness"; then also, "king of Salem" means "king of peace."

3 Without father or mother, without genealogy, without beginning of days or end of life, resembling the Son of God, he remains a priest forever.

Explanation:

- Jesus as the True Melchizedek: This connection to Melchizedek underscores Jesus' eternal and divine priesthood, superior to the Levitical priesthood and fulfilling the role of mediator between God and humanity.

Jesus as the Fulfillment of the Law and Prophets

1. Fulfillment of the Law

Matthew 5:17 (NIV):

"Do not think that I have come to abolish the Law or the Prophets; I have not come to abolish them but to fulfill them."

Explanation:

- Completing the Law: Jesus completes and fulfills the law's requirements through His perfect obedience and sacrificial death, bringing the law to its intended purpose.

- Embodiment of Prophecy: By fulfilling the prophecies, Jesus validates and completes the scriptures, showing that He is the long-awaited Messiah.

2. The New Covenant

Jeremiah 31:31-34 (NIV):

31 "The days are coming," declares the Lord, "when I will make a new covenant with the people of Israel and with the people of Judah.

32 It will not be like the covenant I made with their ancestors when I took them by the hand to lead them out of Egypt, because they broke my covenant, though I was a husband to them," declares the Lord.

33 "This is the covenant I will make with the people of Israel after that time," declares the Lord. "I will put my law in their minds and write it on their hearts. I will be their God, and they will be my people.

34 No longer will they teach their neighbor, or say to one another, 'Know the Lord,' because they will all know me, from the least of them to the greatest," declares the Lord. "For I will forgive their wickedness and will remember their sins no more."

Explanation:

- Internalized Law: The new covenant, established by Jesus, internalizes God's law within believers, transforming their hearts and minds.

- Forgiveness of Sins: Through Jesus' atoning sacrifice, the new covenant offers complete forgiveness of sins, restoring the broken relationship between God and humanity.

Luke 22:20 (NIV):

"In the same way, after the supper he took the cup, saying, 'This cup is the new covenant in my blood, which is poured out for you.'"

Explanation:

- Blood of the Covenant: Jesus' blood seals the new covenant, fulfilling the sacrificial system and establishing a new, enduring relationship between God and believers.

Theological Implications of Jesus' Divinity and Genesis Connection

1. Unified Biblical Narrative

Ephesians 1:9-10 (NIV):

9 He made known to us the mystery of his will according to his good pleasure, which he purposed in Christ,

10 to be put into effect when the times reach their fulfillment—to bring unity to all things in heaven and on earth under Christ.

Explanation:

- Christ-Centered Plan: Understanding Jesus' connection to Genesis highlights the unity and coherence of the entire biblical narrative, with Christ at the center of God's redemptive plan.

2. Assurance of Salvation

Hebrews 10:19-22 (NIV):

19 Therefore, brothers and sisters, since we have confidence to enter the Most Holy Place by the blood of Jesus,

20 by a new and living way opened for us through the curtain, that is, his body,

21 and since we have a great priest over the house of God,

22 let us draw near to God with a sincere heart and with the full assurance that faith brings, having our hearts sprinkled to cleanse us from a guilty conscience and having our bodies washed with pure water.

Explanation:

- Confidence in Christ: The fulfillment of the law and prophecies in Jesus provides believers with confidence in their salvation and direct access to God through Christ.

3. Hope for New Creation

Revelation 21:1-5 (NIV):

1 Then I saw "a new heaven and a new earth," for the first heaven and the first earth had passed away, and there was no longer any sea.

2 I saw the Holy City, the new Jerusalem, coming down out of heaven from God, prepared as a bride beautifully dressed for her husband.

3 And I heard a loud voice from the throne saying, "Look! God's dwelling place is now among the people, and he will dwell with them. They will be his people, and God himself will be with them and be their

God.

4 'He will wipe every tear from their eyes. There will be no more death' or mourning or crying or pain, for the old order of things has passed away."

5 He who was seated on the throne said, "I am making everything new!" Then he said, "Write this down, for these words are trustworthy and true."

Explanation:

- Eternal Hope: The promise of a new heaven and new earth where God dwells with His people provides believers with an unshakeable hope, rooted in Jesus' fulfillment of God's redemptive plan.

Conclusion

Understanding Jesus' divinity and His connection to Genesis is foundational for comprehending the full scope of God's redemptive plan. Jesus, the eternal Word and agent of creation, fulfills the promises and prophecies of the Old

Testament, establishing a new covenant through His sacrificial death and resurrection. This continuity underscores the unity of the biblical narrative and provides believers with assurance of salvation and hope for the future. As we grasp the significance of these truths, our faith is deepened, and our lives are transformed by the power and grace of Jesus Christ, the fulfillment of God's promises from Genesis to Revelation.

Encouragement to Seek a Deeper Relationship with Jesus

As we conclude this journey through the biblical narrative, it is essential to reflect on the significance of seeking a deeper relationship with Jesus Christ. Recognizing Him as the fulfillment of God's promises from the beginning enhances our faith and understanding. This chapter aims to encourage you to pursue a closer walk with Jesus, appreciating His divine nature, His role in creation, and His work in redemption and restoration.

The Fulfillment of God's Promises

Jesus as the Promised Seed

Genesis 3:15 (NIV):

"And I will put enmity between you and the woman, and between your offspring and hers; he will crush your head, and you will strike his heel."

Explanation:

- First Promise: The first promise of a Savior is given immediately after the fall, foreshadowing Jesus' victory over sin and Satan. Recognizing Jesus as the fulfillment of this promise invites us into a story of redemption that spans from the beginning of time.

Jesus as the Fulfillment of the Covenant with Abraham

Genesis 12:3 (NIV):

"I will bless those who bless you, and whoever curses you I will curse; and all peoples on earth will be blessed through you."

Explanation:

- Blessing to All Nations: Jesus, as the descendant of Abraham, brings the promised blessing to all nations. Embracing this truth deepens our understanding of God's faithfulness and His plan for global redemption.

Jesus as the Fulfillment of the Law and Prophets
Matthew 5:17 (NIV):

"Do not think that I have come to abolish the Law or the Prophets; I have not come to abolish them but to fulfill them."

Explanation:

- Complete Fulfillment: Jesus perfectly fulfills the Law and the Prophets, bringing their intended purpose to completion. This fulfillment underscores the continuity of God's plan and the significance of Jesus' mission.

Deepening Your Relationship with Jesus

Pursuing Intimacy with Christ

John 15:4-5 (NIV):

4 Remain in me, as I also remain in you. No branch can bear fruit by itself; it must remain in the vine. Neither can you bear fruit unless you remain in me.

5 "I am the vine; you are the branches. If you remain in me and I in you, you will bear much fruit; apart from me you can do nothing."

Explanation:

- Abiding in Jesus: Jesus invites us to remain in Him, emphasizing the importance of an intimate, ongoing relationship. Abiding in Christ leads to spiritual fruitfulness and a deeper experience of His presence.

Seeking to Know Him More

Philippians 3:10 (NIV):

"I want to know Christ—yes, to know the power of his resurrection and participation in his sufferings, becoming like him in his death,"

Explanation:

- Desire to Know Christ: Paul's passionate desire to know Christ serves as an example for all believers. This pursuit involves understanding the power of His resurrection and sharing in His sufferings, leading to spiritual growth and maturity.

Embracing His Love and Grace

Ephesians 3:17-19 (NIV):

17 So that Christ may dwell in your hearts through faith. And I pray that you, being rooted and established in love,

18 may have power, together with all the Lord's holy people, to grasp how wide and long and high and deep is the love of Christ,

19 and to know this love that surpasses knowledge— that you may be filled to the measure of all the fullness of God.

Explanation:

- Rooted in Love: Being rooted and established in Christ's love enables us to grasp its vast dimensions. Understanding His love fills us with the fullness of God and strengthens our relationship with Him.

The Impact of Recognizing Jesus' Fulfillment

Confidence in God's Plan

Romans 8:28 (NIV):

"And we know that in all things God works for the good of those who love him, who have been called according to his purpose."

Explanation:

- God's Sovereignty: Recognizing Jesus as the fulfillment of God's promises reinforces our confidence in God's sovereign plan. It assures us that He is working all things for our good and His glory.

Living with Hope and Purpose

1 Peter 1:3-4 (NIV):

3 Praise be to the God and Father of our Lord Jesus Christ! In his great mercy he has given us new birth into a living hope through the resurrection of Jesus Christ from the dead,

4 and into an inheritance that can never perish, spoil or fade. This inheritance is kept in heaven for you,

Explanation:

- Living Hope: Our relationship with Jesus fills us with a living hope that transcends circumstances. This hope empowers us to live purposefully, knowing we have an eternal inheritance.

Motivation for Holiness

1 John 3:2-3 (NIV):

2 Dear friends, now we are children of God, and what we will be has not yet been made known. But we know that when Christ appears, we shall be like him, for we shall see him as he is.

3 All who have this hope in him purify themselves, just as he is pure.

Explanation:

- Purity and Holiness: The hope of becoming like Christ motivates us to pursue purity and holiness. Understanding His fulfillment of God's promises encourages us to live in a way that reflects His character.

Practical Steps to Deepen Your Relationship with Jesus

1. Daily Devotion and Prayer

Psalm 1:2-3 (NIV):

2 But whose delight is in the law of the Lord,

and who meditates on his law day and night.

3 That person is like a tree planted by streams of water,

which yields its fruit in season

and whose leaf does not wither—

whatever they do prospers.

Explanation:

- Meditation on God's Word: Regularly meditating on Scripture and spending time in prayer nurtures our relationship with Jesus and strengthens our spiritual roots.

2. Community and Fellowship

Hebrews 10:24-25 (NIV):

24 And let us consider how we may spur one another on toward love and good deeds,

25 not giving up meeting together, as some are in the habit of doing, but encouraging one another—and all the more as you see the Day approaching.

Explanation:

- Encouragement in Community: Engaging in fellowship with other believers provides encouragement, accountability, and opportunities to grow in Christ together.

3. Service and Obedience

John 13:14-15 (NIV):

14 Now that I, your Lord and Teacher, have washed your feet, you also should wash one another's feet.

15 I have set you an example that you should do as I have done for you.

Explanation:

- Following Jesus' Example: Serving others and living in obedience to Jesus' teachings deepen our relationship with Him and reflect His love to the world.

Conclusion

Recognizing Jesus as the fulfillment of God's promises from the beginning enriches our faith and draws us closer to Him. By understanding His divine nature, His role in creation, and His redemptive work, we are invited into a deeper, more intimate relationship with our Savior. This relationship is nurtured through daily devotion, community, and service, all of which lead us to a fuller experience of His love and grace. As we seek to know Jesus more and abide in Him, we are transformed and empowered to live out our calling, reflecting His glory and advancing His kingdom. May this pursuit of a deeper relationship with Jesus bring you joy, peace, and a profound sense of purpose as you walk in the fullness of His promises.

APPENDIX A

Appendix A: Key Biblical Passages Referenced

Genesis

1. Genesis 1:1 (NIV):

"In the beginning God created the heavens and the earth."

2. Genesis 3:15 (NIV):

"And I will put enmity between you and the woman, and between your offspring and hers; he will crush your head, and you will strike his heel."

3. Genesis 12:1-3 (NIV):

1 "The Lord had said to Abram, 'Go from your country, your people and your father's household to the land I will show you.

2 'I will make you into a great nation, and I will bless you; I will make your name great, and you will be a blessing.

3 'I will bless those who bless you, and whoever curses you I will curse; and all peoples on earth will be blessed through you.'"

4. Genesis 14:18-20 (NIV):

18 "Then Melchizedek king of Salem brought out bread and wine. He was priest of God Most High,

19 and he blessed Abram, saying, 'Blessed be Abram by God Most High, Creator of heaven and earth.

20 And praise be to God Most High, who delivered your enemies into your hand.' Then Abram gave him a tenth of everything."

Exodus

5. Exodus 3:14 (NIV):

"God said to Moses, 'I AM WHO I AM. This is what you are to say to the Israelites: 'I AM has sent me to you.'"

6. Exodus 19:5-6 (NIV):

5 "Now if you obey me fully and keep my covenant, then out of all nations you will be my treasured possession. Although the whole earth is mine,

6 you will be for me a kingdom of priests and a holy nation. These are the words you are to speak to the Israelites."

Isaiah

7. Isaiah 53:5-6 (NIV):

5 "But he was pierced for our transgressions, he was crushed for our iniquities; the punishment that brought us peace was on him, and by his wounds we are healed.

6 We all, like sheep, have gone astray, each of us has turned to our own way; and the Lord has laid on him the iniquity of us all."

Jeremiah

8. Jeremiah 31:31-34 (NIV):

31 "'The days are coming,' declares the Lord, 'when I will make a new covenant with the people of Israel and with the people of Judah.

32 It will not be like the covenant I made with their ancestors when I took them by the hand to lead them out of Egypt, because they broke my covenant, though I was a husband to them,' declares the Lord.

33 'This is the covenant I will make with the people of Israel after that time,' declares the Lord. 'I will put my law in their minds and write it on their hearts. I will be their God, and they will be my people.

34 No longer will they teach their neighbor, or say to one another, 'Know the Lord,' because they will all know me, from the least of them to the greatest,' declares the Lord.

'For I will forgive their wickedness and will remember their sins no more.'"

Matthew

9. Matthew 5:17 (NIV):

"Do not think that I have come to abolish the Law or the Prophets; I have not come to abolish them but to fulfill them."

10. Matthew 22:37-40 (NIV):

37 "Jesus replied: 'Love the Lord your God with all your heart and with all your soul and with all your mind.'

38 This is the first and greatest commandment.

39 And the second is like it: 'Love your neighbor as yourself.'

40 All the Law and the Prophets hang on these two commandments."

John

11. John 1:1-3 (NIV):

1 "In the beginning was the Word, and the Word was with God, and the Word was God.

2 He was with God in the beginning.

3 Through him all things were made; without him nothing was made that has been made."

12. John 8:58 (NIV):

"Very truly I tell you," Jesus answered, "before Abraham was born, I am!"

13. John 14:6 (NIV):

"Jesus answered, 'I am the way and the truth and the life. No one comes to the Father except through me.'"

14. John 15:4-5 (NIV):

4 "Remain in me, as I also remain in you. No branch can bear fruit by itself; it must remain in the vine. Neither can you bear fruit unless you remain in me.

5 'I am the vine; you are the branches. If you remain in me and I in you, you will bear much fruit; apart from me you can do nothing.'"

Acts

15. Acts 4:12 (NIV):

"Salvation is found in no one else, for there is no other name under heaven given to mankind by which we must be saved."

Romans

16. Romans 3:25-26 (NIV):

25 "God presented Christ as a sacrifice of atonement, through the shedding of his blood—to be received by faith. He did this to demonstrate his righteousness, because in his forbearance he had left the sins committed beforehand unpunished—

26 he did it to demonstrate his righteousness at the present time, so as to be just and the one who justifies those who have faith in Jesus."

17. Romans 6:4 (NIV):

"We were therefore buried with him through baptism into death in order that, just as Christ was raised from the dead through the glory of the Father, we too may live a new life."

18. Romans 8:1-2 (NIV):

1 "Therefore, there is now no condemnation for those who are in Christ Jesus,

2 because through Christ Jesus the law of the Spirit who gives life has set you free from the law of sin and death."

19. Romans 8:18-21 (NIV):

18 "I consider that our present sufferings are not worth comparing with the glory that will be revealed in us.

19 For the creation waits in eager expectation for the children of God to be revealed.

20 For the creation was subjected to frustration, not by its own choice, but by the will of the one who subjected it, in hope

21 that the creation itself will be liberated from its bondage to decay and brought into the freedom and glory of the children of God."

20. Romans 8:28 (NIV):

"And we know that in all things God works for the good of those who love him, who have been called according to his purpose."

1 Corinthians

21. 1 Corinthians 8:6 (NIV):

"Yet for us there is but one God, the Father, from whom all things came and for whom we live; and there is but one Lord, Jesus Christ, through whom all things came and through whom we live."

2 Corinthians

22. 2 Corinthians 5:17 (NIV):

"Therefore, if anyone is in Christ, the new creation has come: The old has gone, the new is here!"

23. 2 Corinthians 5:20 (NIV):

"We are therefore Christ's ambassadors, as though God were making his appeal through us. We implore you on Christ's behalf: Be reconciled to God."

Galatians

24. Galatians 3:13 (NIV):

"Christ redeemed us from the curse of the law by becoming a curse for us, for it is written: 'Cursed is everyone who is hung on a pole.'"

25. Galatians 3:16 (NIV):

"The promises were spoken to Abraham and to his seed. Scripture does not say 'and to seeds,' meaning many people, but 'and to your seed,' meaning one person, who is Christ."

Ephesians

26. Ephesians 1:9-10 (NIV):

9 "He made known to us the mystery of his will according to his good pleasure, which he purposed in Christ,

10 to be put into effect when the times reach their fulfillment—to bring unity to all things in heaven and on earth under Christ."

27. Ephesians 2:10 (NIV):

"For we are God's handiwork, created in Christ Jesus to do good works, which God prepared in advance for us to do."

28. Ephesians 3:17-19 (NIV):

17 "So that Christ may dwell in your hearts through faith. And I pray that you, being rooted and established in love,

18 may have power, together with all the Lord's holy people, to grasp how wide and long and high and deep is the love of Christ,

19 and to know this love that surpasses knowledge—that you may be filled to the measure of all the fullness of God."

29. Ephesians 4:22-24 (NIV):

22

"You were taught, with regard to your former way of life, to put off your old self, which is being corrupted by its deceitful desires;

23 to be made new in the attitude of your minds;

24 and to put on the new self, created to be like God in true righteousness and holiness."

Philippians

30. Philippians 3:10 (NIV):

"I want to know Christ—yes, to know the power of his resurrection and participation in his sufferings, becoming like him in his death,"

Colossians

31. Colossians 1:15-17 (NIV):

15 "The Son is the image of the invisible God, the firstborn over all creation.

16 For in him all things were created: things in heaven and on earth, visible and invisible, whether thrones or powers or rulers or authorities; all things have been created through him and for him.

17 He is before all things, and in him all things hold together."

32. Colossians 1:27 (NIV):

"To them God has chosen to make known among the Gentiles the glorious riches of this mystery, which is Christ in you, the hope of glory."

1 Timothy

33. 1 Timothy 2:5-6 (NIV):

5 "For there is one God and one mediator between God and mankind, the man Christ Jesus,

6 who gave himself as a ransom for all people. This has now been witnessed to at the proper time."

Hebrews

34. Hebrews 1:3 (NIV):

"The Son is the radiance of God's glory and the exact representation of his being, sustaining all things by his powerful word. After he had provided purification for sins, he sat down at the right hand of the Majesty in heaven."

35. Hebrews 7:1-3 (NIV):

1 "This Melchizedek was king of Salem and priest of God Most High. He met Abraham returning from the defeat of the kings and blessed him,

2 and Abraham gave him a tenth of everything. First, the name Melchizedek means 'king of righteousness'; then also, 'king of Salem' means 'king of peace.'

3 Without father or mother, without genealogy, without beginning of days or end of life, resembling the Son of God, he remains a priest forever."

36. Hebrews 10:1 (NIV):

"The law is only a shadow of the good things that are coming—not the realities themselves. For this reason it can never, by the same sacrifices repeated endlessly year after year, make perfect those who draw near to worship."

37. Hebrews 10:14 (NIV):

"For by one sacrifice he has made perfect forever those who are being made holy."

38. Hebrews 10:19-22 (NIV):

19 "Therefore, brothers and sisters, since we have confidence to enter the Most Holy Place by the blood of Jesus,

20 by a new and living way opened for us through the curtain, that is, his body,

21 and since we have a great priest over the house of God,

22 let us draw near to God with a sincere heart and with the full assurance that faith brings, having our hearts

sprinkled to cleanse us from a guilty conscience and having our bodies washed with pure water."

1 Peter

39. 1 Peter 1:3-4 (NIV):

3 "Praise be to the God and Father of our Lord Jesus Christ! In his great mercy he has given us new birth into a living hope through the resurrection of Jesus Christ from the dead,

4 and into an inheritance that can never perish, spoil or fade. This inheritance is kept in heaven for you,"

1 John

40. 1 John 3:2-3 (NIV):

2 "Dear friends, now we are children of God, and what we will be has not yet been made known. But we know that when Christ appears, we shall be like him, for we shall see him as he is.

3 All who have this hope in him purify themselves, just as he is pure."

Revelation

41. Revelation 1:5 (NIV):

"...and from Jesus Christ, who is the faithful witness, the firstborn from the dead, and the ruler of the kings of the earth. To him who loves us and has freed us from our sins by his blood,"

42. Revelation 21:1-5 (NIV):

1 "Then I saw 'a new heaven and a new earth,' for the first heaven and the first earth had passed away, and there was no longer any sea.

2 I saw the Holy City, the new Jerusalem, coming down out of heaven from God, prepared as a bride beautifully dressed for her husband.

3 And I heard a loud voice from the throne saying, 'Look! God's dwelling place is now among the people, and he will dwell with them. They will be his people, and God himself will be with them and be their God.

4 He will wipe every tear from their eyes. There will be no more death' or mourning or crying or pain, for the old order of things has passed away.'

5 He who was seated on the throne said, 'I am making everything new!' Then he said, 'Write this down, for these words are trustworthy and true.'"

Conclusion

This appendix highlights the key biblical passages referenced throughout the book, providing a foundation for further study and reflection. Each verse contributes to a deeper understanding of Jesus' divinity, His connection to Genesis, and His role in God's redemptive plan. These scriptures encourage believers to seek a closer relationship with Jesus, recognizing Him as the fulfillment of God's promises from the beginning.

APPENDIX B

GLOSSARY OF THEOLOGICAL TERMS

The reconciliation of God and humanity brought about by the sacrificial death and resurrection of Jesus Christ. It involves the concepts of substitutionary sacrifice, satisfaction of divine justice, and restoration of relationship.

Covenant

A solemn agreement between God and humans, often involving promises and obligations. Key biblical covenants include the covenants with Noah, Abraham, Moses, David, and the New Covenant established through Jesus Christ.

Divine Nature

The inherent qualities and attributes that constitute the essence of God. In Christian theology, this term is often used to describe Jesus Christ's divinity, affirming His equality with God the Father and the Holy Spirit.

Eschatology

The study of the "last things" or end times, including the second coming of Christ, the resurrection of the dead, the final judgment, and the creation of a new heaven and new earth.

Exegesis

The critical interpretation and explanation of biblical texts. Exegesis seeks to uncover the original meaning of the text as intended by the author and understood by the original audience.

Incarnation

The doctrine that the Son of God, the second person of the Trinity, became flesh in the person of Jesus Christ. This central Christian belief emphasizes that Jesus is both fully divine and fully human.

Justification

The act of God declaring a sinner righteous on the basis of faith in Jesus Christ. It involves the forgiveness of sins and the imputation of Christ's righteousness to the believer.

Messiah

The "Anointed One" prophesied in the Old Testament, who would deliver God's people. Christians believe that Jesus is the promised Messiah, fulfilling the messianic prophecies of the Old Testament.

New Covenant

The covenant established by Jesus Christ through His death and resurrection, which fulfills and surpasses the Old Covenant. It emphasizes the internalization of God's law, forgiveness of sins, and a personal relationship with God.

Protoevangelium

The term used to describe the first announcement of the gospel in Genesis 3:15, where God promises a future Redeemer who will crush the head of the serpent, symbolizing victory over sin and Satan.

Redemption

The action of saving or being saved from sin, error, or evil. In Christian theology, it specifically refers to the work of Jesus Christ in securing salvation for humanity through His death and resurrection.

Restorative Justice

A concept of justice focused on the restoration of relationships and community healing rather than merely punishing wrongdoing. In the context of Jesus' ministry, it involves bringing spiritual, physical, and social healing.

Revelation

The act of God revealing Himself and His will to humanity. This can occur through general revelation (nature, conscience) and special revelation (Scripture, Jesus Christ).

Sacrifice

The offering of something valuable for a higher purpose or in atonement for sin. In the Christian context, it refers to Jesus' sacrificial death on the cross as the ultimate atonement for humanity's sins.

Salvation

Deliverance from sin and its consequences, granted by God's grace through faith in Jesus Christ. It encompasses justification, sanctification, and glorification.

Sanctification

The process by which believers are made holy, set apart for God's purposes. It involves spiritual growth and moral transformation through the work of the Holy Spirit.

Trinity

The Christian doctrine that God exists as three persons in one essence: the Father, the Son (Jesus Christ), and the Holy Spirit. Each person is fully God, yet there is one God.

Typology

A method of biblical interpretation in which an element found in the Old Testament is seen to prefigure one found in the New Testament. For example, the story of Joseph is seen as a type of Christ.

Word (Logos)

A term used in John 1:1 to describe Jesus Christ as the preexistent, divine Word through whom all things were created. The Logos embodies divine reason and creative order.

Conclusion

This glossary provides definitions of key theological terms used throughout the book. Understanding these terms enhances comprehension of the theological concepts discussed and facilitates deeper study and reflection on the biblical narrative and the person and work of Jesus Christ.

APPENDIX C

FURTHER READING AND STUDY QUESTIONS

To deepen your understanding of the topics covered in this book, the following resources are recommended. These books and articles provide further insights into the divinity of Jesus, His fulfillment of the law, and His central role in God's redemptive plan from Genesis to Revelation.

1. Books on the Divinity of Jesus

   - "The Case for Christ" by Lee Strobel

   - "Knowing Jesus Through the Old Testament" by Christopher J.H. Wright

   - "Jesus and the Eyewitnesses: The Gospels as Eyewitness Testimony" by Richard Bauckham

2. Books on Biblical Theology and Fulfillment

   - "The Drama of Scripture: Finding Our Place in the Biblical Story" by Craig G. Bartholomew and Michael W. Goheen

- "The Mission of God: Unlocking the Bible's Grand Narrative" by Christopher J.H. Wright

- "From Eden to the New Jerusalem: An Introduction to Biblical Theology" by T. Desmond Alexander

3. Books on Jesus in the Old Testament

- "Jesus on Every Page: 10 Simple Ways to Seek and Find Christ in the Old Testament" by David Murray

- "The Shadow of Christ in the Law of Moses" by Vern S. Poythress

- "God's Big Picture: Tracing the Storyline of the Bible" by Vaughan Roberts

4. Books on New Creation and Eschatology

- "Surprised by Hope: Rethinking Heaven, the Resurrection, and the Mission of the Church" by N.T. Wright

- "The New Creation: John Wesley's Theology Today" by Theodore Runyon

- "Heaven: A Comprehensive Guide to Everything the Bible Says About Our Eternal Home" by Randy Alcorn

5. Commentaries and Study Bibles

- "The NIV Application Commentary Series" by various authors

- "The ESV Study Bible"

- "The New Bible Commentary" edited by D.A. Carson, R.T. France, J.A. Motyer, and G.J. Wenham

Study Questions

These study questions are designed to facilitate deeper reflection and discussion on the themes and concepts presented in this book. They can be used for individual study, small group discussions, or as prompts for further research and writing.

1. Understanding Jesus' Divinity

- What are the key biblical passages that affirm Jesus' divinity, and how do they contribute to our understanding of His nature?

- How does the concept of the Trinity help explain Jesus' relationship with the Father and the Holy Spirit?

2. Jesus in the Old Testament

- How does the promise of the seed in Genesis 3:15 foreshadow Jesus' victory over sin and Satan?

- In what ways does the life of Joseph prefigure the life, death, and resurrection of Jesus?

- How does Melchizedek serve as a type of Christ, and what is the significance of his priesthood?

3. Fulfillment of the Law and Prophets

- What does it mean that Jesus came to fulfill the law and the prophets? How does this understanding impact our view of the Old Testament?

- How does the New Covenant, established by Jesus, differ from the Old Covenant? What are its key features?

4. Redemption and New Creation

- How does Jesus' death and resurrection fulfill the requirements of the law and provide redemption for humanity?

- What is the significance of the new creation in the life of a believer, and how does it relate to the ultimate renewal of all things?

5. Living in Light of Jesus' Fulfillment

- How can believers cultivate a deeper relationship with Jesus, recognizing Him as the fulfillment of God's promises?

- In what practical ways can believers live out the principles of restorative justice in their communities?

- What role does hope play in the life of a believer, and how does the promise of the new creation influence daily living?

6. Biblical Interpretation and Application

- How does understanding typology enhance our reading of the Old Testament and its connection to the New Testament?

- What are the benefits of conducting exegesis and using resources like Strong's Concordance in Bible study?

7. Personal Reflection

- Reflect on a time when a deeper understanding of Jesus' role in God's plan significantly impacted your faith. How did it change your perspective or actions?

- How can you apply the teachings of this book to your daily life and spiritual growth?

Conclusion

This appendix provides additional resources and questions to help you delve deeper into the themes explored in this book. By engaging with these materials and reflecting on the study questions, you can enhance your understanding of Jesus' divinity, His fulfillment of God's promises, and His transformative impact on your life. May your study lead to a richer, more intimate relationship with Jesus Christ and a deeper appreciation of His central role in God's redemptive plan.

BIBLIOGRAPHY

BOOKS ON THE DIVINITY OF JESUS

1. Bauckham, Richard. Jesus and the Eyewitnesses: The Gospels as Eyewitness Testimony. Eerdmans Publishing Co., 2006.

2. Strobel, Lee. The Case for Christ. Zondervan, 1998.

3. Wright, Christopher J.H. Knowing Jesus Through the Old Testament. InterVarsity Press, 1992.

Books on Biblical Theology and Fulfillment

4. Alexander, T. Desmond. From Eden to the New Jerusalem: An Introduction to Biblical Theology. Kregel Publications, 2009.

5. Bartholomew, Craig G., and Michael W. Goheen. The Drama of Scripture: Finding Our Place in the Biblical Story. Baker Academic, 2004.

6. Wright, Christopher J.H. The Mission of God: Unlocking the Bible's Grand Narrative. InterVarsity Press, 2006.

Books on Jesus in the Old Testament

7. Murray, David. Jesus on Every Page: 10 Simple Ways to Seek and Find Christ in the Old Testament. Thomas Nelson, 2013.

8. Poythress, Vern S. The Shadow of Christ in the Law of Moses. P&R Publishing, 1991.

9. Roberts, Vaughan. God's Big Picture: Tracing the Storyline of the Bible. InterVarsity Press, 2002.

Books on New Creation and Eschatology

10. Alcorn, Randy. Heaven: A Comprehensive Guide to Everything the Bible Says About Our Eternal Home. Tyndale House Publishers, 2004.

11. Runyon, Theodore. The New Creation: John Wesley's Theology Today. Abingdon Press, 1998.

12. Wright, N.T. Surprised by Hope: Rethinking Heaven, the Resurrection, and the Mission of the Church. HarperOne, 2008.

Commentaries and Study Bibles

13. Carson, D.A., R.T. France, J.A. Motyer, and G.J. Wenham, eds. The New Bible Commentary. InterVarsity Press, 1994.

14. The ESV Study Bible. Crossway, 2008.

15. The NIV Application Commentary Series. Zondervan, various authors and dates.

Articles and Papers

16. Blomberg, Craig L. The Historical Reliability of the Gospels. InterVarsity Press, 2007.

17. Carson, D.A. "Christ and Culture Revisited." Reformation and Revival Journal, vol. 12, no. 3, 2003.

18. Kostenberger, Andreas J., and Richard B. Gaffin, Jr. The Glory of God. Crossway, 2010.

Theological Dictionaries and Encyclopedias

19. Elwell, Walter A., ed. Evangelical Dictionary of Theology. Baker Academic, 2001.

20. Ferguson, Sinclair B., and David F. Wright, eds. New Dictionary of Theology. InterVarsity Press, 1988.

Online Resources

21. Blue Letter Bible. "Strong's Concordance." Blue Letter Bible, www.blueletterbible.org.

22. Bible Gateway. "Bible Commentaries." Bible Gateway, www.biblegateway.com/resources/commentaries.

23. The Gospel Coalition. "Resources on Biblical Theology." The Gospel Coalition, www.thegospelcoalition.org/topics/biblical-theology.

Conclusion

This comprehensive bibliography provides a wide range of resources for further study on the divinity of Jesus,

His connection to the Old Testament, and His fulfillment of God's redemptive plan. These sources include books, commentaries, articles, and online tools that will enhance your understanding and deepen your faith. Use these materials to continue exploring the profound truths about Jesus Christ and His central role in the biblical narrative.